# What Do You Really Want?

Trust and Fear in Decision Making
at Life's Crossroads and in Everyday Living

**MAGGID**

Shayna Goldberg

# What do you *really* want?

TRUST AND FEAR
IN DECISION MAKING
AT LIFE'S CROSSROADS
AND IN EVERYDAY LIVING

Maggid Books

*What Do You Really Want?*
*Trust and Fear in Decision Making*
*at Life's Crossroads and in Everyday Living*

First edition, 2021

*Maggid Books*
*An imprint of Koren Publishers Jerusalem Ltd.*

PO Box 8531, New Milford, CT 06776-8531, USA
& PO Box 4044, Jerusalem 9104001, Israel
www.maggidbooks.com

The publication of this book was made possible
through the generous support of The Jewish Book Trust.

Hardcover ISBN: 978-1-59264-571-8

Printed and bound in the United States

To our next generations,

Dalya, Cheli, Liad, Netanel,
Ronya, Jack, Benny, and Boaz

May you continue to carry the torch of Torah
and be the next link in the eternal chain

Abba and Mommy

Laad – Jewish Leadership Fund

❧ ❧ ❧

Dedicated in loving memory of

Mayer Penstein
מאיר יוסף בן אברהם ויתה

Devoted husband, father, and grandfather

Abba showed us by example how to lead lives guided by Torah in the
modern world. He made his values and convictions perfectly clear and
instilled them in his children and grandchildren, all while giving us the
strength and confidence to make decisions on our own. He taught us
that when approached from a Torah perspective, even life's most difficult
challenges become experiences through which we can learn and grow.
We miss him and his guidance more every day, but hope to live up to
his example.

Mina Penstein
Rivkie & Lance Hirt          Chani & JJ Hornblass
Shulamit & Avi Penstein     Shoshana & Avi Mizrachi
and families

*In honor of*

## Judah and Shayna Goldberg

*and all their tireless work on behalf of Torah and Am Yisrael.*

*Donny and Arielle Rosenberg*

❧ ❧ ❧

*In loving memory of our fathers and Zadie and Saba,*

## Rabbi Jonas Hochman *z"l*
## Noé Gidali *z"l*

*Barbara and Simcha Hochman,*
*David and Ayelet Ellenbogen, and Ariel and Amalia Hochman*

❧ ❧ ❧

*In honor of our three wonderful daughters:*

## Sara Schnaidman Gillers
## Ayala Schnaidman Glass
## Malka Schnaidman

*who have all benefited from Shayna's insights and wisdom.*

*Menachem and Rena Schnaidman*

We are honored to play a role
in making Shayna's wisdom accessible to young and old alike.
May she continue to lead us all in personal and spiritual growth.

Jordana and Kalman Schoor and family

❧ ❧ ❧

לעילוי נשמת
הרב אברהם יואל בן פנחס

❧ ❧ ❧

In appreciation of our parents

Debby a"h and Maurice a"h Friedman

and

Barbara and Manfred a"h Joseph

who taught us the importance of supporting Torah education
for our children and grandchildren and who demonstrated and modeled
for us a steadfast commitment and unwavering dedication
to the continuity of our Mesorah.

Paula and Howard Friedman

In honor and appreciation of Shayna Goldberg
for teaching and continuously guiding our daughters
who were her students at Migdal Oz, and by extension our entire family.

With much gratitude.

Jennifer and David Ottensoser
Lily (2015)
Molly (2018)

Dedicated by Dassi and Joey Silverman
in honor of Shayna Goldberg
for being a tremendous role model to our daughter.
May you continue to spiritually inspire young women
for many years to come.

In recognition of Shayna Goldberg's impactful work
with the women of Migdal Oz,
and in honor of her mother, Abby Lerner,
for her work on behalf of geirei tzedek and so many others in need.

Robin and Joshua Rochlin

In recognition of and appreciation for

Shayna Goldberg

for her extraordinary devotion, tireless dedication
and unwavering commitment to her students,
the schools in which she has taught
and the communities in which she has lived.

Her outstanding character and integrity is an inspiration and example
for all who value and cherish living by Torah ideals.
מחיל אל חיל!

Rivi and Avi Katz

# Contents

Preface: How This Book Came About and for Whom It Is Intended ......xi

Acknowledgments.................................................xv

Introduction: "And the Main Thing Is to Have No Fear at All" ........xxi

### PART I: THE ROLE OF TRUST IN
### PERSONAL DECISION MAKING

1. Common Fears in Decision Making............................... 3
2. Elements of Good Decision Making..............................21

### PART II: DECISION-MAKING CASE SCENARIOS

3. Introduction to Case Scenarios .................................. 35
4. School Choices.................................................. 37
5. Career Options ................................................. 41
6. Aliya .......................................................... 47
7. Use of Time ................................................... 53
8. Personal Finances.............................................. 57
9. Therapy....................................................... 61
10. Religious Observance........................................... 65
11. Dating and Relationships ...................................... 73

12. Engagement . . . . . . . . . . . . . . . . . . . . . . . . . . . . . . . . . . . . . . . . . . . . . . . 85

13. Having Children . . . . . . . . . . . . . . . . . . . . . . . . . . . . . . . . . . . . . . . . . . . 93

14. Divorce . . . . . . . . . . . . . . . . . . . . . . . . . . . . . . . . . . . . . . . . . . . . . . . . . . . . 95

15. Adult Children . . . . . . . . . . . . . . . . . . . . . . . . . . . . . . . . . . . . . . . . . . . . . 99

16. Retirement . . . . . . . . . . . . . . . . . . . . . . . . . . . . . . . . . . . . . . . . . . . . . . . . 105

**PART III: EMPLOYING TRUST IN EVERYDAY LIVING**

17. Raising Children with Trust. . . . . . . . . . . . . . . . . . . . . . . . . . . . . . . . . . .111

18. Mentoring and Educating with Trust. . . . . . . . . . . . . . . . . . . . . . . . . .119

19. Sharing Trust in Friendships and Relationships . . . . . . . . . . . . . . . .131

20. Trust in Ourselves . . . . . . . . . . . . . . . . . . . . . . . . . . . . . . . . . . . . . . . . . .137

**PART IV: AFTER THE DECISION ... NOW WHAT?**

21. Developing Confidence in Our Decisions. . . . . . . . . . . . . . . . . . . . . . . 145

22. Living with Tension . . . . . . . . . . . . . . . . . . . . . . . . . . . . . . . . . . . . . . . . .151

Conclusion: Get Out There and Live! . . . . . . . . . . . . . . . . . . . . . . . . . . . . .155

# How This Book Came About and for Whom It Is Intended

When I decided to become a teacher, I imagined the classes that I would prepare, the skills that I would attempt to help students develop, the content that I would discuss, and the lifestyle that I would model. Already at the time, I anticipated that forming deep and meaningful relationships with students would be a fulfilling and significant part of the job for me – something that would hopefully develop naturally along the way. Eighteen years later, I can say with certainty that the relationships that I have been privileged to cultivate with so many students have been the most rewarding part of my career. Many of them have extended well beyond these students' years in the classroom and have evolved into mutual friendships, as these young women have matured into the finest of adults.

Admittedly, I didn't realize early on what these relationships would entail and the vast amount of time that would be spent on and invested in personal conversations. While these conversations span lots of different topics and issues, a certain pattern emerged. I began to take note of how many of them centered around big decisions that had to be made by someone who was feeling confused and was in search of direction and advice during the decision-making process.

Earlier in my career, these conversations would terrify me. I was not sure what my role was. I certainly did not want to make a decision for someone; I did not want that responsibility. More importantly, I believe deeply in personal autonomy and in each individual charting his or her own life course. Acute awareness of these two issues led me to naturally shy away from trying to directly influence people's decisions, and instead, toward guiding them to figure out what they wanted for themselves.

In doing so, I found myself thinking about what constitutes a good decision, as well as reflecting on decisions that my husband and I made for ourselves. In retrospect, there seemed to be some key components that had helped us figure out what we wanted when we reached a crossroads and had to make a significant decision. For us, these components have often provided insight into how to proceed, and, over time, I have found myself sharing them in conversations with students and peers. In these pages I will do my best to describe the components that we have found to be helpful in our lives and in the lives of others.

Many of our major life decisions happen in our earlier years, as we decide where to study, what career to pursue, and with whom we want to build a life. They may also include questions such as where to settle down, when to start a family, and how many children to have. In this sense, this book focuses on a population most commonly between the ages of eighteen and forty-five, which often finds itself in the throes of weighty decisions at many different crucial intersections of life. A lot of the examples given throughout the book relate most directly to the first half of that age bracket, as developing trust in our ability to make good decisions during those early adult years is especially important.

However, I believe the relevance of this book is by no means limited to a younger age group. There are major decisions that continue to challenge us in middle age and beyond. These might include thoughts about a possible career change, a troubled marriage, a looming retirement, or relationships with grown children and grandchildren. There are also ongoing decisions that we all face throughout our lifetimes with regard to how we spend our money or use our time, when professional counseling should be pursued, how we interact with family members, and what attitude toward religious observance we want for ourselves.

My hope is that this book can be helpful, in different ways, for individuals at any stage of life. For a younger cohort, it provides concrete tools for those on the brink of major decisions who might feel stuck about how to proceed. For someone who has already made many of life's big decisions, it may help them articulate instincts and intuitions, positive and negative, that are often difficult to verbalize. The language of this book may enable some readers to better understand why they look back on some decisions with regret or resentment, regardless of the consequences, while other decisions have left them feeling empowered and energized. These insights can provide clarity that not only helps us interpret our past but also allows for better understanding and self-awareness in the future.

Finally, this book is intended to be a resource for anyone counseling others who need to make decisions. Teachers, administrators, therapists, counselors, friends, spouses, and, perhaps most significantly, parents and grandparents are often consulted and asked to weigh in and share thoughts and guidance with students, clients, campers, children, and grandchildren who seek their advice on some significant and important decision. Beyond specific chapters about parenting and educating with trust, case scenarios (either fictionalized or shared with permission, with names changed) that cover a spectrum of life situations and decisions may shed light on the different factors and fears that often arise as someone contemplates what he or she wants. Understanding these factors more deeply and thinking about them from the inside may enable us to better guide and direct another toward a good decision.

Given all that, I will reiterate that this is not an academic or scholarly work, but rather a presentation of ideas that reflect only my own thoughts and experiences about elements that I have found to be helpful in decision making. As the main theme of this book is developing trust in one's intuition, I would encourage anyone for whom this book does not resonate to follow their own instincts and search for and rely upon alternative approaches that speak to and work for them. At the same time, it is my hope that this book can be informative and helpful in empowering each of us to make our own decisions from a place of trust, rather than fear, and that it provides tools to help us guide others to do so as well.

# Acknowledgments

It was my husband, Judah, who first introduced me to the language of trust and fear when we were dating. From that time on, we found ourselves referencing it often and thinking about why trust and fear are, indeed, often dichotomous emotions. As we began our journey through life together, it became a cornerstone of our educational approach, regarding both our children and our students. Over the years, we have had many conversations about its implications in our own lives and in the lives of others.

It was also Judah who initially raised the idea of my writing this book and who continued to encourage me over the last several years to see it through. While the book may be written in my voice and illustrate many of the interactions I have had during years of teaching and mentoring, in reality it is a joint project that Judah has been heavily invested in throughout. Judah is always there to support me in everything I do, and there is no piece of writing that I ever publish without him reading it over, sharpening it, and improving it in numerous ways. His patience and attention to detail far exceed mine, and his ability to find just the right way to express a complicated thought always impresses me. Both the content of this book and its presentation have been influenced and shaped by his thoughtfulness, precision, emotional intelligence, dedication, humility, and insight. His many hours of editing were a labor of love, and his touch can be felt in every sentence of the book. I feel blessed to have a partner in life whom I trust so deeply. I genuinely feel that *sheli shelo* – with regard to this book and everything else I am involved with in life. Our most meaningful and significant endeavor together has been raising our precious children: Shmuel, Elyashiv, Akiva, Netanel, and Tzofiya. When I look at them and I see how they reflect Judah's values, intelligence, passion, commitment, and sensitivity, I feel for all of us that *ashreinu ma tov ḥelkeinu*.

I am grateful to the many friends, mentors, students, and relatives who read drafts of this book and offered me their feedback. Their insights, critiques, and perspective helped refine the content in numerous ways.

From the moment I sought his professional opinion, Reuven Ziegler, editorial director at Koren Publishers Jerusalem, provided me with encouragement and direction. His initial enthusiasm enabled me to imagine that my vision for this book could be realized and gave me the strength to invest my all into developing the manuscript.

My thanks also to Matthew Miller, publisher of Koren, and the multiple staff members of Maggid Books with whom I have had the pleasure of working. I could not have asked for a better editor than Caryn Meltz, who oversaw every detail of this project from beginning to end. I am indebted to Tani Bayer for her creativity and patience in designing the beautiful cover. It has also been truly wonderful to work with Aryeh Grossman, Debbie Ismailoff, and Dvora Rhein. Each of these individuals excels in their professional roles and are the finest of people to engage with personally.

I am overwhelmed by the generosity of the couples who helped make the publication of this volume possible. Many of them I first met when I was privileged to teach their incredible daughters in Maayanot Yeshiva High School in Teaneck, New Jersey, or the Stella K. Abraham Beit Midrash for Women of Yeshivat Har Etzion (Migdal Oz) – or both! Others are friends with whom

I have collaborated in the pursuit of shared ideals and visions. All of them are dear to me, and I am grateful for their moral and financial support.

Dr. David Pelcovitz, a renowned psychologist whose reputation precedes him, is also a close family friend, and I feel blessed that he read an early version of this book and so graciously shared with me ways to give more context to its content. His support for and belief in the project meant a lot to me and gave me the confidence to forge ahead with it, even during some of the more challenging moments.

Dr. Tovah Lichtenstein, an esteemed lecturer and social worker, offered pointed critique and insight which allowed me to better formulate whom the book is meant for, what it can offer, and what its limitations are. I am so appreciative that she took the time to read through an early draft and offer her feedback.

My cousins Dr. Jennie Goldstein, a well-known psychiatrist; Bracha Krohn, a master educator; and Aliza Shapiro, a talented social worker, all read the book thoroughly and used their expertise and experience to suggest little tweaks, as well as more significant additions and reformulations that enhanced the content, relatability, and presentation of the manuscript. I feel so grateful to have family members who are also such wonderful friends and whom I respect so much.

My nieces, nephews, and first cousins' children responded with delight to my requests to read the manuscript, and their comments ensured that the book would be relevant to and resonate with young adults. A special thank-you to Ruthie and Ephraim Goldstein and Rachelli Pearl, whose specific recommendations made a real difference in the formulation of several sections of the book.

I am lucky to share deep friendships with multiple talented and experienced educators whose encouragement and input were invaluable for this project. Leora Bednarsh took a particular interest in the topic of the book and helped push me to share these ideas in writing. Leora happily read a few different drafts and offered suggestions that made a significant contribution to the final product.

Dena Rock encouraged me to better develop some of the crucial sections of the book. Her questions prodded me to think more carefully about how to describe some of the concepts and present them more clearly.

Mali Brofsky helped me fine-tune some important formulations. Her insights as an experienced and perceptive social worker were greatly appreciated.

Laurie Novick read a final draft of the book and offered some concrete suggestions for how to both sharpen and flesh out various ideas. Laurie's attention to detail and her years of teaching and writing made her comments particularly valuable and impactful.

Rachel and Aminadav Grossman are former students who have become colleagues and the dearest of friends. I am grateful that they each took the time to read the book and share with me their thoughts. It has been many years now that we have been discussing these themes together, and these candid conversations have been very meaningful to me and influenced the development of the ideas presented here.

Indeed, this book is a product of numerous conversations with many students over the last eighteen years. I have been blessed to teach the finest young adults, who are thoughtful, insightful, ambitious, and committed. They have pushed me hard with their questions and have forced me to think carefully and with nuance about issues in education. It is through working with them and being privy to their thoughts, struggles, and aspirations that the approach in this book has been explored, tested, and honed in real life in a spectrum of circumstances. The relationships that I have been privileged to develop with so many special and extraordinary young women are among the most cherished in my life. Although I could not mention each of you by name, I wrote this book with you in mind, as your lives and your decisions have provided me with enormous personal inspiration.

I am grateful to the SKA Beit Midrash for Women of Yeshivat Har Etzion (Migdal Oz) and its *rosh beit midrash*, Rabbanit Esti Rozenberg, for taking a risk, just ahead of my aliya, and inviting me to play a part in its educational mission and vision. The *beit midrash* is a place that encourages, believes in, and thrives on a trust-based educational philosophy, and I feel fortunate to be part of its vibrant and rich spiritual community.

Racheli Schmell has been a partner, colleague, and among the closest of friends for almost ten years. Beyond the day-to-day work that we do together in the *beit midrash* of Migdal Oz, we share an incredible bond of understanding and mutual respect. Most of the ideas in the book I have discussed and processed with Racheli, and her emotional intelligence, sensitivity, love, and support have been guiding forces in my own personal and professional development since we made aliya.

One of the most significant blessings of meeting Judah was becoming part of the Goldberg family. From the early days of our marriage, my siblings-in-law, Daniella and Joseph Hellerstein and Rabbi Efrem and Yocheved Goldberg, have been true confidants and friends. We have the best time together, laughing and enjoying each other's company, both on our own and with all our terrific and entertaining children. Most meaningfully, they are always incredibly supportive and have been there for us with love and dedication in both wonderful and difficult times.

My in-laws, Murray and Basheva Goldberg, shower me with their love and attention and are exceedingly proud and supportive of the various projects and initiatives in which I take part. I have learned so much from their Shabbat table, their *hakhnasat orḥim*, their *ḥesed* and *tzedaka*, and their never-ending devotion to every member of their immediate and extended family. May they be blessed with many more healthy and happy years together.

My three sisters, Hudi Elsant, Havi Bitter, and Sefi Hefter, have always been my closest friends. From the time we were little girls and had weekly Friday night sleepovers, we have confided in each other about everything and have been through it all together. My sisters are my greatest cheerleaders and my most honest critics. This book has benefited enormously from their careful reads and reflections upon it. They shared with me both small and major recommendations that greatly enhanced the content. I am in awe of each of my sisters and the amazing wives, mothers, and professionals that they are. I am boundlessly grateful for the depth of the relationships that I share with each of them and that Judah and I share as a couple with my sisters and brothers-in-law, Nachman, Elichai, and Jonathan, and their precious children.

My parents, Rabbi Yaacov and Abby Lerner, may not have used the formulation "trust and fear" when they raised my sisters and me, but everything in our upbringing reflected the incredible trust that my parents have in Hashem, in the inherent goodness of people, and in us, their children. They taught us to trust ourselves and our instincts and to rely heavily on our intuition. They raised us to have self-confidence in who we are and what we believe and to be strong and independent thinkers. It is they who always encouraged me to think about "What do you really want?" and it this underlying and enveloping spirit that I hope I am able to bring to life and concretize in this book.

As this project reaches completion, I am overflowing with gratitude to the *Ribbono shel Olam* for the opportunities He has presented me with over the course of my life. I daven that Judah and I, along with our children, will always have the wisdom to use the *berakhot* He has bestowed upon us in meaningful and significant ways.

*Introduction*

# "And the Main Thing Is to Have No Fear at All"

W hen I was very little, I learned a song to the well-known words of Rabbi Nachman of Breslov: *Kol haolam kulo gesher tzar meod,* "The whole wide world is a very narrow bridge." These words illustrate the harsh reality that sometimes we feel and experience "the whole wide world" as an overwhelming, dangerous, precarious, and risky place to live. In this epigram, fear is acknowledged directly and not denied. And yet, Rabbi Nachman ends the quote by reminding us that *veha'ikkar lo lefaḥed klal,* "the main thing is to have no fear at all." Fear, although natural and normal, will often inhibit us from accomplishing our goals. Fear can stand in the way of what we know to be true and necessary. Fear can stop us from doing what we feel we want to do and should do.

Back when we were a newly married couple – and faced with lots of decisions – my husband recalled an article from an old *Jewish Action* magazine (Summer 1989) by Dr. Mordechai Breuer, where he discusses the educational philosophy of his great-grand-father, Rabbi Samson Raphael Hirsch. There was one line that stood out for my husband and which led to many conversations about the kind of teachers and parents we hoped to become: "In education let ourselves be guided by trust and truth, not by fear" (p. 8).

Rabbi Hirsch believed that the opposite of fear is trust. Trust, however, unlike fear, is unfortunately not something we always feel instinctively. Fear is naturally the more powerful and dominant emotion, perhaps because at times it serves the important role of protecting us, both emotionally and physically. If something is even the slightest bit threatening to us, we feel that fear and are programmed to react. Sometimes, though, we are overly sensitive to our fears, and we can resort to them too quickly and let them dominate too easily. When this happens, we can find ourselves overwhelmed, depressed, and incapable of moving forward. When we are guided by trust, on the other hand, it is incredibly empowering and motivating.

In my teaching, I have tried to emphasize these concepts and, in doing so, have come to realize how many people struggle to develop trust in themselves. This challenge seems to confront today's younger generation in particular, and there may be specific reasons why.

Much research has been done over the last couple of decades regarding changing trends in our society that affect our ability to trust ourselves and our choices. The research suggests that it has become harder for young people to confidently rely on their instincts. Instead, they often become paralyzed as they contemplate how to advance.

One factor is that we live in a world that inundates us with endless options, and narrowing them down to figure out what we want can be a harrowing task. Moreover, the more choices we have before us, the less satisfied we often feel with our decisions. In his 2004 book, *The Paradox of Choice: Why More Is Less,*

Dr. Barry Schwartz describes how we have not seemed to benefit psychologically from the greater freedom and autonomy that is available. It becomes especially difficult to own, take responsibility for, and be happy with our choices when we see so many alternative options surrounding us.

Furthermore, our contemporary pluralistic environment teaches us to accept and embrace a wide range of different ideas and approaches. This ethic of tolerance and respect, especially dominant in universities and certainly laudable in many ways, can sometimes leave us feeling hesitant to make even the most basic decisions when we feel that they might include inherent judgments about the options we are turning down. What might it say about me and my opinions if I make this specific choice and not another one? What does it mean regarding how I think about others who have made that choice? In a 2014 *New York Times* essay, "My So-Called Opinions," Zachary Fine, then a junior at New York University, raised this issue when he asked: "How does the ethos of pluralism inside universities impinge on each student's ability to make qualitative judgments outside of the classroom, in spaces of work, play, politics, or even love?"

Other studies document evolving changes in parenting and their effects on children's decision-making abilities. Over time, we have moved from a more authoritarian form of parenting, where "father knows best" and would sometimes harshly discipline in order to instill values, clear standards, and obedience in his children, to a style of parenting that is much more relaxed and permissive – sometimes to the point where the parent struggles to assert authority and the child is less certain about what is wanted from him.

In addition, there has been an increasing trend to hover over children and to shield them from encountering obstacles and challenges as they grow up. In 1990, Foster Cline and Jim Fay in their book, *Parenting with Love and Logic,* coined the term "helicopter parents" to describe parents who oversee every aspect of their children's lives in whatever way they can to ensure their children's success at school, at camp, in social situations, and even at work. While this style of parenting may yield more immediate, quantifiable results, children may never develop the instincts to make their own good decisions or fend for themselves.

More recently, in a 2019 *New York Times* essay, "How Parents Are Robbing Their Children of Adulthood," Claire Cain Miller and Jonah Engel Bromwich used the term "snowplow parent" to describe a parent who proactively tries to make sure that a child never encounters pain, difficulty, or failure. This approach appears to be rooted in fears of potential negative consequences for children who are exposed to hardship. Ironically, however, children of snowplow parents are often less resilient and have trouble dealing with frustration and solving problems independently. They can experience greater struggles developing the maturity and confidence needed to trust themselves and to make good decisions on their own. Moreover, in the long run, fear will inevitably play a large role in decision-making when trust in oneself is lacking.

In summary, while developing self-confidence has never been simple, the challenge has been magnified by an abundance of choice, an emphasis on pluralism, and current trends in parenting. The need to educate toward and encourage trust has never been greater.

This book explores a range of situations in which I have encountered the benefits of a "trust" approach to decision making. In my experience, when people are taught to trust themselves and their deepest and truest instincts, as well as to trust the world around them, they almost always make better decisions and end up happier and more satisfied and fulfilled as a result. The "trust versus fear" dichotomy is one that echoes throughout every area of life. In my own life experience and as a parent and educator, I have seen the effects that employing trust over fear can have, and I am hopeful that readers of this book may benefit similarly as well.

# PART I

# The Role of Trust in Personal Decision Making

## Chapter 1

# Common Fears in Decision Making

Throughout life, we are faced with a myriad of decisions. There are the big decisions that will affect the trajectory of our lives, such as where to study, whom to marry, what career to pursue, and where to live; and there are small ones, such as how to spend the day, what clothing to wear to a job interview, whom to invite as company for Shabbat lunch, or what to make for dinner. Any decision can be an unpleasant experience if we find ourselves doubting the way that we reached our conclusions. Wouldn't it be wonderful, then, if we could trust ourselves to make good decisions?

Before we can discuss how to trust ourselves and what elements might contribute to good decisions, we need to first examine some of our most common fears and explore how they can often get in the way of making the best possible decisions. When decisions are motivated from a place of fear, it becomes much more difficult to take responsibility for them – especially when the outcome is not the one we hoped for. There can be resentment, frustration, and even anger at the situation that we never really desired and only found ourselves confronting because we made a decision from a place of fear rather than following our intuitive sense of what we wanted. That resulting anger with ourselves and others leaves us less able to own the decisions we make and to move forward in a positive and healthy way.

In addition to concrete, narrow fears that stem from specific concerns about the options that face us, there are some broader, underlying fears that can often get in the way of making good decisions. Presented here are a few of the most common ones, which can manifest themselves in a variety of ways at different points in life.

## OUR SELF-PERCEPTION/IMAGE WILL BE AFFECTED

We each have our own narrative surrounding how we think of ourselves and how we make sense of our personal stories. Based on that narrative, we create a framework that can heavily influence the way that we approach our decisions.

### Bracha: Overachiever

*Bracha, a medical student, had always been an overachiever who pushed herself hard and was often overworked and stressed as a result. When she began to date, most young men that she met were of a similar nature. When Hillel was suggested to her by a good friend, she was taken aback and even offended. Hillel was known to be a wonderful person, but he was a fifth-grade teacher in a local day school. Bracha could not even imagine beginning a relationship with someone who she rashly assumed had little professional ambition. "I'm the kind of person who of course is going to marry someone who is a serious intellectual. That's so defining as to who I am," she thought to herself. "How could anyone even think that Hillel could be right for me?"*

Our preconceived notions of ourselves play a strong role in dictating what options we are willing to consider:

*"Of course, someone like me who loves Israel so much has to make aliya."*

*"I am the kind of person who is destined to have a high-powered job."*

*"I always know what I want. If I've been dating her for a few months and I'm still not sure, she must not be the one."*

*"I am independent and strong. There is no way I would benefit from therapy."*

But have we stopped for a minute to give ourselves room to think?

*Do you actually want to make aliya?*

*Do you want to go into that specific profession?*

*Do you really want to break up with her?*

*Do you want to work through this difficulty completely on your own?*

Who decides what is appropriate and not appropriate for us? Shouldn't we decide for ourselves in the moment and not be boxed in by how we self-identified a year or two ago, or even last week? Don't we want to leave room for what we feel, deep inside, might be right for us right now, even if it somehow does not jive 100 percent with the picture we have constructed of ourselves?

## Sam: Passionate Zionist

*From the time he was in high school, Sam knew that he wanted to make aliya. When it came time to choose a yeshiva in Israel, he specifically chose a hesder yeshiva, where it was not uncommon for American students who come to study for a year or two to then make aliya and join the Israeli program. After making aliya and being drafted into the Israeli army with his yeshiva friends, Sam found himself deliberating over whether to complete his service after fifteen months as scheduled or whether he should stay on and enroll in an officers' training course.*

*For as long as he could remember, Sam had been a passionate Zionist who was committed to giving his most to his precious country. He believed that it was important to serve in any way he could. He had even successfully convinced some of his friends who were wavering that they should make aliya and join the army. Didn't that mean that there was no other choice for him but to become an officer?*

In conversation with Sam, it became clear that although he thought that continuing in the army was intrinsic to what it means to be a true Zionist, he did not actually want to give more of his time. His army experience was challenging – physically, emotionally, and religiously. He was happy that he had enlisted and served, but he was ready to move on and head back to civilian life. As soon as Sam understood that not becoming an officer did not necessarily mean that he cared less about Israel or that he was weak and was just choosing the more comfortable option, he was able to make the decision that was best for his overall situation.

Other people's concept of who we are can also influence our self-perception and affect our decision making.

**Noam: Major League Player**
*Noam was a bright high school senior who did well in school and took his religious life seriously. In thinking about what yeshiva he wanted to attend in Israel, he felt torn between an established, well-known institution that for years had attracted motivated young men like himself, and a new, much smaller yeshiva that offered more of the kind of learning he enjoyed and wanted to pursue. When he shared his dilemma with his teachers, one after the other would respond with various retorts: "But you are a major league player; you belong in a major league school!" "How can someone like you even consider that yeshiva?" After hearing this so many times, Noam was left feeling that if he was going to be true to who he was, he had only one option, which was to attend the bigger and more established yeshiva, even though his heart was pulling him in the other direction.*

Noam enrolled in the larger yeshiva and regretted his decision throughout his time spent there and beyond. He has lingering resentment toward his teachers, who never stopped to really listen to him and hear what he was saying, and he harbors anger and frustration toward himself for not trusting his own instincts.

## WHAT OTHERS WILL THINK

What others think of us not only influences our self-image but can also sway our decisions in one way or another, even when we know that it is a mistake to let that happen.

### Daniel: Settling?

*Daniel had been dating Esther for a while and was very happy whenever they spent time together. Esther was caring, sensitive, understanding, and an all-around wonderful person. But he knew that his friends and family thought he could do better and that he was settling for the first girl he felt good about. Daniel didn't think so. He felt fairly confident that he and Esther had built a beautiful relationship and would continue to do so. He was also mature enough to realize that as soon as the week of sheva berakhot was over, life would go back to routine and no one would care anymore about the new couple. All that would matter, at that point, would be their own happiness. In fact, he knew that his friend Mark, who had married "a major catch," was miserable in his day-to-day life with her. And yet, Daniel was still struggling to move forward, as he dreaded the subdued reactions that he would have to endure after they announced their engagement.*

### Karen and Aryeh: Irresponsible?

*Karen and Aryeh were a young married couple who were both still in school. Most of their married friends were open about the fact that they were using birth control and would continue to do so for some time until life had settled down and it made more sense to consider having a baby. Karen and Aryeh had discussed birth control when they were dating and* had come to the conclusion that they both felt ready to have children. While school was taxing, they were used to juggling a lot in their lives, and they also both worked and made enough money to be able to support a baby. After much thought and conversation, they knew that this is what they wanted. Having a baby did not scare them; they felt ready to be parents. But they were nervous about how everyone around them would react. They were pretty sure that their friends would think they were crazy and that their parents would think of them as irresponsible.

### Gila and Aaron: Traitors?

*Gila and Aaron lived in a community where most couples in their close-knit circle of friends sent their children to the same elementary school. They and many of their friends were active members of the board and PTA. Gila and Aaron had happily sent their oldest three children to the school, and they had been pleased both with the education and the overall experience. But their fourth child, who would be entering first grade in the fall, had some unique learning needs, and Gila and Aaron had not felt satisfied with how the school had addressed them in pre-K and kindergarten. They knew that another local school was known for having a wonderful resource room and for providing exceptional resources for children with unique needs. They began deliberating if they should switch their son out of his current school and enroll him there instead. They both felt that would be best for him, but they were consumed by worry over how their friends would view their decision and if it would be seen as a betrayal of the school on whose behalf they had all worked so hard.*

Should these types of concerns influence our decisions when we feel confident about what we want?

#### IS THIS NORMAL?

People like to think of themselves as mainstream and "normal." We like our reactions and behaviors to fit within accepted societal norms, and we judge ourselves by whether what we are experiencing, thinking, and feeling are "normal," by which we mean typical, expected, and accepted by people similar to ourselves. "Feeling normal" gives us a sense of relief that we are OK. It allows us to be confident that what we are experiencing is par for the course. If we don't feel that way, we may fear that something is wrong, and that can affect our decision making.

### Hannah: Unfazed, Until...

*Hannah hung up the phone feeling shaken. Her best friend Maya's husband had to travel for business for a week, and Maya had just confided in her about how awful it was to be apart from him. She sounded absolutely distraught. A few weeks earlier, though, Hannah's husband had to return to the Israeli army for two weeks. While it had been tough and she had missed him, she had made it through OK and had found other ways to busy herself and to use her time productively. Now she was plagued with doubts about her relationship. Was it normal that she had managed their time apart decently? What did it mean that she had not been distraught the way Maya was? What did it say about her marriage?*

We never really know what is going on in other people's lives. Every individual both processes and expresses emotions differently. While Hannah should be honest with herself about why she is so disturbed by Maya's comments, Hannah should not judge her own relationship by what she interprets to be normal based on Maya. In this situation, the concern that she is "not normal" can lead her to come to conclusions and make decisions that she does not really want.

Sometimes the opposite can occur. The very fact that we are feeling normal can stop us from trusting our instincts.

### Dina: First-Time Mother

*Dina was a first-time mother. She loved her baby dearly and could not get over how intense her feelings were for him. When she was home with him, she spent a lot of time holding, playing with, and snuggling* with him. *The older he got, the cuter he was. He was playful, interactive, and all-around adorable. Lately, though, something felt off to her. He didn't seem to be as active as usual, and his movements seemed heavier and more laden with difficulty. When she asked her mother about it, her mother brushed it off and told Dina that she had always been a worrier. Her friends, who had kids of similar age, told her that it was normal for children to go through different phases and that nothing she was describing seemed too worrying. Even the pediatrician didn't seem concerned; but Dina was not certain they were right. She felt that they had been at the pediatrician on a better day and that the doctor had not seen the baby at his worst.*

Dina's gut told her that she should take her baby to a specialist, but she was afraid of what she would find out and have to deal with. Most of all, she was scared that she would go from being a typical mother of a typical kid to something "not normal," and this fear prevented her from trusting her instincts and acting on them.

### FEELING UNSETTLED/LOSING A SENSE OF CLOSURE

Most of us enjoy feeling settled. We like having a sense of control about where our lives are headed and certainly don't want to needlessly rock the boat. Therefore, when we do find ourselves at a crossroads and in a state of uncertainty, it is typical to want to resolve that as quickly as possible. It is an uncomfortable place to be. Wanting to avoid this stage of uncertainty can therefore sometimes prevent us from allowing ourselves to consider making decisions that could take us in new directions. Alternatively, it can also push us to make decisions before we are ready. There is an urge in us to know where we are headed, even if the situation is premature.

### Yosef: Too Quick to Commit

*At the beginning of Yosef's year in Israel, he was already toying with the idea of deferring college further and staying for another year in Israel. He loved the environment that he was in and felt confident that he would want to be there for a second year. Despite his teachers telling him that he did not need to make a decision about the following year until March, Yosef wanted to know what he was doing so that he would not have to spend the next five months stressing over the decision. He told all of his friends what his plans were. As the year progressed, though, thoughts would creep into Yosef's mind that maybe he had decided too soon. He began to feel that maybe he had made the wrong decision. But he wasn't sure. In addition to the embarrassment that he would have to face when he told his friends and teachers, he also did not want to reenter that state of uncertainty. He felt that he had made a decision and should stick with it.*

So many fears are affecting Yosef's decision. He is afraid to feel unsettled, and that leads him to make a decision before he is ready to. And then, on the other hand, he is reluctant to consider making a new decision once he has closure because he does not want to return to that place of uncertainty. He is also worried about what his friends and mentors will think of him. But if Yosef is honest with himself, he will consider the fact that he does not really have genuine closure. Though he is trying his best to deny it, he is already in limbo. He is unsure if he wants to stay for *shana bet*, and it would not be wise to force himself to make the decision final before he knows what he really wants.

## Abigail and Reuven: Desperate to Move

*Abigail and Reuven were desperate to move. For some time they had felt that their family had outgrown their modest home and that they would all benefit from additional space. They had already been in touch with a real estate agent and had looked at several houses, but each time they were disappointed to discover that the house was not a viable option. One morning, they finally saw a house that appealed to them, was in the right neighborhood, and approached their price range. "Let's make an offer!" Abigail said the minute they got into the car. Reuven knew that in order to maintain a strong negotiating position, they needed to play this smart and not appear too eager. But Abigail was so nervous that they would lose it. She pressured Reuven to make an offer that very night.*

Abigail knew intuitively that Reuven's approach was correct, but she desperately wanted and needed a sense of closure. She was anxious to know what the future held. She so badly wanted to move, and she was eager to jump on the first option that looked like a realistic possibility. Ironically, her very need to feel settled might jeopardize their ability to get the house that they want to settle down in.

## HAVING TO ADMIT A MISTAKE AND FACE "WASTED" TIME AND RESOURCES

It is always hard for us to admit our mistakes. It is even harder when we feel that we have "wasted' a considerable amount of time, money, or energy. The fear of having to shift course, start over, and deal with past events can hamper us from making the decisions that we want to.

### Brian: "Who Drops Out of Law School?"

*Ever since he was a young boy, Brian knew that he wanted to be a lawyer. Whenever he would spend time with his father at his law firm, he found the cases his father was involved with to be fascinating. Deciding to be pre-law in college was as obvious to him as his food preferences. He "just knew" that that was what he was drawn to and wanted to do with his life. Interning for a lawyer over the summer further contributed to his sense of certainty. From the time that Brian began law school, however, he had not been himself. He was stressed all the time and was not enjoying the studies. Areas that had once interested him suddenly seemed boring. It was hard to study for exams. There was so much information and little motivation. Brian missed interacting with people and having time to pursue other interests in his life. Older classmates had told him that he would get used to the grind, but his first year of law school was coming to a close, and that was not the case. He had not fully appreciated what the field of law entailed and was no longer sure that he wanted to practice it. But how could he leave? Who drops out of law school? Could that even be done?*

*Beyond the fear of what others would think, Brian felt lost. Who was he, if not a future lawyer? What would he do with his life? All of these fears ate away at him, but perhaps the greatest fear of all was the thought that all these years had been a waste. He had spent so much time in high school investing in the mock trial team. He had studied hundreds of hours for the LSATs and had interned for multiple lawyers, and for what? He would never be able to recover that lost time and money. He was also terrified of having to start over from scratch. He would need to find a new career and go back to square one. Maybe that alone was a reason to stay in law school.*

In life we can come to a crossroads where we need to think about how we want to move forward. If it becomes clear to us that we are looking toward a path that is different from what we previously assumed we would follow, it can be hard to change course. It is not easy to leave behind all the steps we took to propel us forward on the trajectory that we have been on. But the decisions that we made in the past should not hamper us from making the best decisions that we can in the present and for the future. Often, our sense of having wasted time and resources demonstrates a lack of perspective; most often we needed to walk that path in order to become the person we are and to arrive at the new turning point we now face. In any case, all we can do at any given time is make the best next decision we can, given all the information that we have at the moment.

In dating relationships, in particular, the fear of wasting time, resources, and energy can affect a decision in either direction. One can feel that one should end a relationship before one is ready to because of the fear of "wasting" any more time. Alternatively, individuals sometimes stay in a relationship when they know that they should break up because they are afraid to admit that the time they've invested thus far has not brought them any closer to settling down. Denial, though, doesn't change that reality, nor does procrastination. At least we can take solace in knowing that every relationship builds us into who we are and helps us understand what we want and need from a life partner.

Coming back to Brian – should he quit law school? Not necessarily. He needs to weigh a lot of factors, including the challenges of setting out on a new path. But the fear of swallowing lost time should not be one of them.

## MISSING AN OPPORTUNITY

When we think about different options lying before us, we might fear passing up on one that seems like an opportunity which will never present itself again. Even if we might be leaning toward one option or feel with certainty that it is best for us, the fear that we might miss out on something and regret this may push us to choose an option that is different from what we really want.

*"I think I want to start college, but maybe I should stay for shana bet because it is a once-in-a-lifetime opportunity to learn Torah for another whole year."*

*"I don't really want to make aliya as a single, but if I don't, I may never integrate or know Hebrew as well."*

*"I like the man I am dating, but I have not had the opportunity to date much and see what other options are out there."*

*"I think I am happy in my marriage, but what if I could be happier?"*

The truth, though, is that whatever decision is made, an opportunity will be lost. Inherent in decision making is choosing one option and shutting the door on another. Although someone might feel like *shana bet* or aliya at a young age can be a wonderful opportunity, the question, Is this what you want? cannot be avoided. If there is a feeling that this is an opportunity that we really want to seize, then we should go right ahead and make the most of it. But if we realize that a fear of missing out (FOMO) is driving the decision, then we may need to step back and reassess.

**HAVING REGRETS**

A corollary of the fear of missing opportunities is the fear of having regrets. When we settle on one course of action, we may be not only concerned about missing out on the alternative, but also worried that, in retrospect, we will doubt our decision and have to deal with lasting negative feelings.

### Yael: "Am I Being Irresponsible?"

*Yael's mind would sometimes race when she was not feeling well. If she had a headache, she wondered whether she had a brain tumor or aneurysm. If her chest hurt, perhaps she was having a heart attack, and various small birthmarks always got her thinking about skin cancer. It's not that she was a hypochondriac; she had enough self-awareness and medical insight to know that she was probably fine. Yet she found herself worrying about the consequences of not being more assertive for herself, her husband, and her children. The doctor's reassurances sounded reasonable, but was it responsible for her to rely on his assessment and just move on? "Should I see a specialist? Should I get an MRI?" she would wonder. But the question that plagued her most was, "Am I going to regret that I did not look into this further? Will I look back on this and feel like I handled these decisions irresponsibly, for myself and for my family?"*

More than her fear of being sick, Yael is worried about dealing with potential lingering feelings of regret over her decisions to not seek further testing. This fear of future regrets can arise whenever we find ourselves making any decision that contains some inherent risk.

*"What if we decide to go on a vacation and something happens to our child while we are away? Will we regret having left her?"*

*"What if I go skiing and get injured? Will I feel foolish that I went?"*

*"What if I do not pursue a job offer that has some great perks? Will I feel dumb afterward?"*

These kinds of thoughts are natural and understandable and probably should give any of us pause before we proceed with a course of action. But should they singlehandedly dissuade us from what intuitively makes sense for us? Furthermore, what is the alternative? To avoid any risk of possible regret under any circumstances? What price would we then pay in terms of giving up all that we really want for ourselves (and our loved ones!), including the ability to function without constant worry?

Inevitably, all we can do is make good decisions, with openness and honesty about the risks involved and how much we are willing to bear. Beyond that, the rest is in God's hands. We can never succeed in eliminating all risk from our lives, but we can at least aim to make decisions that we can embrace with confidence and clarity. Even if things go wrong, we will know that we deliberated and chose responsibly, which is all that we (and God) can ever ask of ourselves. The antidote to regret, I think, is not avoidance of hard decisions, but the opposite – confronting them directly with levelheadedness, humility, and trust.

### SELF-NEGATION

One of the more complex fears we might encounter is the fear that we are negating a feeling or thought we may have by not considering it seriously enough in our decision-making process. We should trust ourselves, however, to know how to appropriately weigh our different thoughts and feelings as we balance them in our everyday lives.

### Ezra: Productive Enough?

*Ezra, at the age of eighteen, was an extremely disciplined young man. He made calculated and thoughtful decisions about how to spend his time and he was able to get a lot done each day. And yet, often at the end of the day, a thought would enter his mind that he had not been productive enough. Ezra knew in his heart that the thought was irrational. He could point to multiple concrete daily accomplishments, but at the same time he would still think that maybe he could have done more. While his gut told him to trust himself that he had had a good day and should go to sleep feeling satisfied, he was afraid that he was denying the voice within him encouraging him to do one last task before heading to bed. When Ezra allowed this fear to get the best of him, he would feel good and productive in the moment but would then always regret staying up late.*

Over time, Ezra learned to trust himself and his gut feeling that he should go to sleep. Instead of allowing his thoughts to frighten him, he began to engage them by actively balancing them with his awareness of all that he had accomplished. Instead of negating them, he accepted them as a part of his thought process and of who he was. He realized that even when he had a particular dominant thought in his head, he could still actively choose to make a different decision.

Ora came to a similar conclusion in her own situation.

### Ora: Protecting Her Needs

*Ora was a forty-six-year-old mother of four wonderful but demanding teenagers. She felt that she was constantly being asked for one thing or another. One evening, Ora was in the middle of working at her computer when her sixteen-year-old daughter interrupted her and asked to be driven to the movie theater, where she would meet up with a friend. Ora felt the anger welling up inside her. "Does she not see that I'm working? Is she the only one who has needs in this family? Are my needs not important to anyone here?" She feared that no one took her and her endeavors seriously.*

*Ora was about to share these thoughts out loud, but then she paused and thought for a moment. Ora knew that she was sometimes overly sensitive to and easily triggered by people ignoring her needs. Growing up as the youngest sibling of two brothers who were much older, she would often be schlepped along to activities that were not suitable for her age. Those experiences in childhood had left a deep impression on her.*

*Once Ora acknowledged this, she was able to think about her situation differently. Instead of living in fear that she was forever being taken advantage of by her children, she realized that their requests were appropriate to ask of a mother. She trusted that if she ever felt that someone was crossing a line and legitimately not respecting her needs, she would be able to recognize that and tell them. At the same time, she did not need to allow that fear to get in the way of good and responsible parenting.*

If we consider our thoughts and feelings, engage them, account for them, and then decide how best to proceed, there is no reason to fear that we are negating a part of ourselves. Rather, we can trust that we have made good decisions about how to balance our various thoughts and emotions.

## FAILURE/REJECTION

Sometimes fear of failure is what stops us from moving forward with a decision that we want to make.

### Asher: More Than Capable

*Asher was a successful high school teacher who was well liked by his students and who had managed to accomplish all of the professional goals that he had set for himself in his teaching. But lately, he had been feeling that he was ready to move on to a position that demanded more of him and that made fuller use of his many talents. Without pursuing anything, he was offered to be the principal of a nearby yeshiva day school, whose board had done a search and had discovered Asher on its own. Asher was intrigued by the offer for many reasons, but he was hesitant to take it. He was so comfortable in his teaching job. He knew what it took to succeed, and he knew that he made a difference in the lives of his students. What if he failed as a principal? What if he didn't really have what it takes to* be an effective administrator? Deep down, the anxieties seemed irrational, but he considered declining the offer just to make them go away.

Although Asher knew that he was ready and wanted to move on to a more demanding professional role, and he was aware of the fact that being a principal appealed to him, the prospect of failing was so daunting that it clouded his thinking and made him extremely hesitant to make the leap.

At times our fear of failure comes not in the form of failing at a task, but, rather, feeling rejected in a relationship. That, too, can stop us from making the decisions that we want to make.

### The Heller Family: Navigating New Friendships

*The Heller family had recently moved to a new community, where they were greeted warmly by their neighbors. Many families invited them for Shabbat meals, and slowly the Hellers began to feel more integrated into their new group of friends. There was one family, though, that left them feeling confused about the nature of their relationship. When they accepted an invitation for a Shabbat meal at the Stein family, they had a wonderful time together and saw it as the beginning of a close connection. After a couple of years, however, the Hellers realized that despite the fact that they had hosted the Steins several times, the Steins had never reached out again. Mr. and Mrs. Heller really liked the Steins and wanted to invite them to their daughter's upcoming bat mitzva. They worried, though, that maybe the Steins were just being polite but had no real interest in pursuing this relationship, and they feared that their efforts would be rejected. In the end they decided not to invite them, so as not to face the fact that they might not come. After the fact, they regretted that they had let this fear of rejection influence them.*

The fears discussed here are understandable. It makes sense why they arise, but ultimately, they prevent us from thinking about what we really want. Any time we are facing a decision, big or small, it can be helpful to consider if one of these general fears is clouding how we process it.

*Chapter 2*

# Elements of Good Decision Making

Having reviewed the role of fear in decision making, we can now explore some of the elements that can be helpful in coming to decisions that we can trust and feel good about. Trust means listening to our inner voice. Trust means stepping back from pros-and-cons lists and asking ourselves, *"But what do I really want?"* Moreover – *"Do I want this even though all the considerations on paper might objectively point in a different direction?"*

But what does it mean to "want" something? I wish to be clear about this point:

**Doing what we want does not mean making an impulsive decision based on a strong, overwhelming feeling of desire. Rather, doing what we want means paying close attention to a deep, intuitive feeling that rises up within us over time and pushes us in a certain direction, despite the fact that it might surprise us or others.**

Often a person can experience different levels of want. **When I refer to "want" in this book, I refer to the deeper, more significant desires that we have for ourselves.**

*In the moment, I may want to stay in bed and pull the covers back over my head, but at the same time I know that what I really want on a deeper, more meaningful level is to get up, start my day, and be productive.*

*In the moment, I may want to respond to my boss with a sharp retort, but I know that overall I am happy at my workplace and want to keep my job.*

*In the moment, all I want to do is eat the cheesecake that is sitting on my counter, but I also know that I want to eat well and feel good about my health.*

Listening to those deeper desires may entail denying what we want in the moment, but it is a recognition that sometimes transient feelings and desires overwhelm and overpower what it is we know we really want in the long term. Having the strength to ignore those short-term desires is actually a display of trust in what we want for ourselves in the big picture.

In order to make decisions based on what we want for ourselves in the long run, it is important to make sure that our choices line up with our core values. In chapter 20, we will discuss in detail what it means to have core values and how to use them in ways that help guide our decisions in life.

When we follow our intuitions and decide to do something because we have reflected carefully upon it and trust our sense about how we should proceed, then we will be more ready and willing to take responsibility for our decisions.

Over time, I've identified several elements that define and underlie good decisions:

1. **Researching/collecting information** with regard to our options

2.  Extreme **honesty** regarding consequences, hesitations, and fears on both sides of the decision

3.  Focusing only on the **best next decision** that can be made and not letting factors that we can't know now get in the way and cloud our judgment

4.  Making sure that our decision is **not motivated by fear**

5.  **Trusting** our deep self-awareness of **what it is we really want**

These elements may contribute to a decision-making process that does not necessarily unfold in a linear manner. For example, someone may find herself thinking about her fears before she has narrowed down her considerations to the best next decision she faces or before she has even finished doing her research and collecting all the necessary information. One may also find that some of these elements do not naturally resonate or feel necessary in his or her personal process. These elements, therefore, are not steps to be checked off, but components that can be helpful in formulating a decision made from a place of trust, even if the process sometimes occurs in a more natural, intuitive manner.

Let's take a closer look at each of these elements.

## 1. Researching/collecting information with regard to our options

It is hard to make a good decision without having a very clear and full sense of the different choices. Sometimes when we find that we are having trouble with a decision, it can be simply because we don't have enough information about the different options, as well as what their implications will be. The first potentially helpful element of any decision, therefore, is researching and collecting information.

This may sound obvious, but so often we waste time and energy worrying prematurely about decisions that we haven't yet investigated thoroughly enough, or about which information is not yet fully available. Sometimes we spend a lot of time thinking about a decision that isn't immediately relevant, and, therefore, it is difficult to accurately know and explore now what will be important to us later. When, however, we research our options well, specifically at the time that a decision needs to be made, the resulting confidence can be exactly what we need in order to make it from a place of trust.

To offer a simple example, in choosing between two different careers, one needs to know what each of those careers actually involves. This could mean talking to people who work in each of those jobs, reading about the work, and observing it up close by shadowing someone who works in each field. We would probably also want to find out what the schooling and training process is really like, as well as the potential compensation.

Often, just understanding more deeply what different options entail can be enough to clarify the decision. Once we have more information, it is possible that one of the options will be naturally more or less appealing than the other and what we want will be more obvious. Sometimes, however, the research stage only makes the decision harder and more complex. We find out that there are appealing and unappealing aspects on both sides of the equation.

In those situations, we might be tempted to think that further research and exploration – including consulting with mentors or spiritual leaders – will always resolve the problem. We might want to imagine that there is one option that is objectively right and one that is wrong, one option that is morally correct or superior and one that is less so, or, in the perspective of some, one option that is *ratzon Hashem* (the will of God) and one that is not, and if we can only figure out which option is the "right" one, we will know what to do.

I have found, though, that most decisions that we have to make in life are not decisions between right and wrong, good and bad. If the options were so starkly different, then there would be no genuine decision to be made, just a truth to uncover. Moreover, if there is really one objectively better and right choice that everyone would agree is preferred, then at some point we would imagine that it would become glaringly obvious to all.

The significant decisions of our lives, however, are almost always between two options which are right or good in different ways, or which appeal to us from different perspectives or for different reasons. This is true not only with regard to little decisions such as which kind of coffee to order or which shoes to buy, but even for huge, weighty, and more agonizing decisions such as whether or not to make aliya, have another child, or stay married. In these cases, there is rarely an objectively right decision. But thinking with honesty about issues of trust and fear can help guide us to make a good decision for ourselves.

Decisions can be especially stressful and challenging if we think we are searching for the one morally correct option or the single choice that is consistent with the will of God. That perspective inherently brings with it an external pressure to meet an undefined standard. The vast majority of times, however, there are multiple legitimate options, and the task remains the same one as always – to figure out what we think is the best next thing to do at that juncture in time. While decisions may indeed involve significant moral or religious considerations, the challenge is usually in weighing and balancing competing values or impulses and figuring out how best to resolve those conflicts.

Finally, different individuals may employ divergent languages to talk about the decisions in their lives, but I find that the underlying issues are often remarkably similar – as in this interaction.

## A Personal Story: *Ratzon Hashem?*
*Years ago, I needed to decide if I should leave my husband and children in Israel for a few days to attend the brit mila of my new nephew in America. I thought carefully about the decision, weighed all the*

*different factors, and decided to make the trip. While I knew that, on the one hand, I value my roles as a wife and a mother and care deeply about providing for my family, I also knew how much it would mean to my sister for me to be there with her, and I was really excited about spending time with her and her family and attending the simḥa. A part of me felt that it was a selfish decision to travel on my own, especially when I was well aware of how much anticipation I felt. But I also knew that I was not just going out of personal desire, but out of dedication to my sibling. I carefully considered the values at stake on both sides and thought about what I wanted to do in light of them.*

*At the time, I was talking to a close friend of mine in Israel who was similarly deliberating over whether or not to attend the wedding of a friend of hers in America. When I asked her what was preventing her from going, she said that she was struggling to figure out what ratzon Hashem is in this situation. Would God prefer that she celebrate with her close friend in America or stay home and be there for her family? A few days later, she told me she had decided to make the trip. When I jokingly asked her if God had spoken to her, she replied that after much thought, she realized that Hashem would want her to be at the wedding.*

I remember remarking to my friend at the time that even though the language we use may not be the same, I do not think that our thought process was much different. She reviewed her options, decided what she thought was right based on her values and understanding of God's will, and called it *ratzon Hashem*. I also reviewed my options considering my values, including my religious priorities, and decided what I thought was the right thing to do. I owned the decision as mine, and hoped, too, that it would find favor in God's eyes, knowing full well that there is no way to ever know with certainty if it did.

If we take all of our values (including religious and moral ones) into account when making a decision, we can trust that our deep intuition will guide us to a "good" decision for ourselves, though not necessarily the exclusively "right" one.

2. **Extreme honesty regarding consequences, hesitations, and fears**

Once a lot of information has been collected, the idea of creating a pros-and-cons list can be an appealing and useful way of organizing our thoughts. We can write down or compose a mental list of all the pros and cons of one decision versus all the pros and cons of the other.

It is good to be aware, however, that unless the only goal is to see which option has the greater number of either pros or cons, such a list does not usually prove to be too helpful as a tool in making a final decision. If the aspiration, though, is to honestly explore all of the fears and hesitations that one has about a particular decision, then this exercise can serve a very important role. Can we honestly think through all of our concerns about each option? Can we put into words what we are nervous about? Do we understand and accept the realities of the different sides of the equation? Only when we can express our fears honestly and lay them all out on the table can we begin to think about our true options.

Sometimes the fears that we feel are less about the specific options and more connected to internal ambivalence. It may become apparent that there are underlying issues that must be addressed, relationship dynamics that need to be explored, or past experiences that need to be confronted, either on our own or with outside help. When we can work through those components and then acknowledge all options as real possibilities despite our fears, it allows us to better examine honestly what we are truly after and what we really want.

An important component of this honesty with oneself is being honest about our non-negotiables. Everyone should have concerns in life that are so important to them that they are not up for discussion. These can be core values, ideals, or concrete practices. They are the lines that we don't want to cross or the elements that we want to be always present in our lives no matter what. In any decision that we make, it is important to consider if the decision is taking these non-negotiables into account and allowing us to stay true to who we want to be.

### 3. Focusing only on the best next decision that can be made

It can be incredibly helpful to remember to focus on the specific decision at hand. Our deliberations should surround only the immediate decision that we have researched and collected information about. All we can do at any given moment is focus on the imminent choice that stands before us and make the **best next decision** that we can. We cannot make decisions that are further down the line and about which we are not yet fully informed. But if we consistently make one good decision after another, this will hopefully lead us to where we want to be. Furthermore, while thinking and stressing about the long term often leaves us feeling confused and unequipped, when we focus only on the next decision that we need to make, we often find that we have all the tools to respond appropriately. Part of trusting ourselves is trusting that at every given stage, we will know how to navigate our way to the next one.

### 4. Making sure our decision is not motivated by fear

If we have done all of our research, collected all of the information we need about our different options, thought about and considered honestly all of the possible fears and hesitations at stake, and zoned in on what specific, immediate decision needs to be made right now, then we can consider if **fear** is what is motivating how we will choose to proceed. Fears, while always important to take into account, should not lead us to a place where we feel that we are not in control of our choices. The overwhelming emotion of fear should not be the entire basis of any final decision.

A risk or danger concerning one option can often legitimately lead us to prefer the alternative. But ultimately, we should feel that we are making a positive decision to pursue the option that is right for us following all of our deliberations. It should resonate within us that we are choosing something that we want rather than running away from the option we are drawn to but afraid of.

## A Personal Story: Shopping at Tzomet HaGush

*After a spate of terror attacks at the Gush Etzion Junction, I found myself feeling scared to shop in the stores in that area. Even though the big and cheap local supermarket at the junction was the place I most frequently bought my groceries, I suddenly no longer had an interest in shopping there. I felt paralyzed with regard to how to move forward. I knew that I could start shopping in the smaller mini-markets within the different local yishuvim and that I would feel safer knowing that everyone had to pass through multiple layers of security in order to gain entry. However, those markets were much more expensive and did not have as wide of a selection.*

*There were a few times that I forced myself to go down to my regular supermarket (with pepper spray in hand), because I did not want to succumb to my fear. It was a difficult and challenging experience, as I did not enjoy picking out my fruits and vegetables while looking over my shoulder, concerned about a possible stabbing. Eventually I made the decision to stop shopping there. It just was not pleasant for me, and I realized that I wanted to go elsewhere.*

While the fear of terror attacks was the most significant factor in this decision, I did not feel that it overwhelmingly got in the way of my doing something I was drawn to. Rather, I deliberately decided that I *wanted* to shop in stores where I felt more comfortable. This distinction makes all the difference.

There are significant and legitimate concrete fears that may heavily influence our decisions. Someone may decide not to go rock climbing with their friends because of the risks, not to enter small spaces because of claustrophobia, or not to drive through a neighborhood known to be dangerous. But in each situation, the person has made a calculated decision about what risk or discomfort he or she is willing to bear and has not let the emotion of fear overwhelm and dominate the ability to own the ultimate choice. What is crucial is that we feel good about our decision and confident that it is the one that we proactively chose, are ready to move forward with comfortably, and own and take responsibility for. It is knowing that we are doing what we ultimately want to do, as opposed to allowing our fears to control us.

## 5. Trusting what we want

The final stages of decision making are where trust is at play. Once we have thought a lot about the elements above, we can stop talking, analyzing, and researching and let ourselves pay careful attention to what we are feeling. Trust requires deep personal honesty and self-awareness. For some, this seems natural and familiar, while for others, this may be a new skill to develop. If we are not willing to be honest with ourselves about how we are feeling, though, it is hard to develop trust in ourselves. If, on the other hand, we are willing to listen to our instincts, then at some point we will most likely develop a deep, intuitive sense of what it is we want to do. Trust means believing that what we feel makes sense for us – after a thorough and honest decision-making process – is also what we should do.

Being able to fully trust ourselves and have confidence in what we want often takes time. Even after we have researched and thought a lot about our decision, it can still take days or weeks or more for our brain to make sense of and organize everything we are thinking, and for our heart to recognize and be attuned to what we are feeling. But when we stop analyzing the decision and start paying attention and listening closely to what our inner voice is saying, we will hopefully find the answer to the question of what it is that we want.

We should not be afraid to give ourselves however much time we need to make a good decision. We should trust that we know how to guide ourselves to good things and that, if we are allowed space and the time to listen to ourselves, we will find clarity in our decisions. In a situation where there is an external pressure of a deadline by which a decision needs to be made, it can be helpful to stop talking about, stressing over, and analyzing the various factors a few days before that point so that we will have the ability to focus and hear our inner voice before the deadline. When we stop constantly thinking about the decision, the answer often wells up within us and gives us a sense of clarity and certainty.

Occasionally, however, the process of coming to a decision takes more than just time. What we fear, what we trust, and what we want are all dynamic and can evolve with deep personal introspection and growth. Furthermore, for lots of different reasons based on our past and our present, identifying these elements of fear, trust, and wants and separating between them might not be so easy, even after silent reflection. Sometimes a decision involves exploring and resolving deeper conflicts that are behind the root tensions we are feeling. Decision making is not always exclusively based on rational thought processes. There can be multiple layers of decision involved in one looming choice, and a person may need to first set out on a journey of self-exploration, either on one's own or with a professional, of underlying ambivalence, pain, or doubts that he or she is experiencing before a conclusion can be reached. The components outlined above may not always be the only steps that are necessary to move forward, and part of trusting ourselves is also trusting an instinct that it would be important and helpful to explore this dilemma more deeply in order to figure out what it is we want.

However, even though we can learn and even aspire to want something different for ourselves than what we want at the present moment, I would still contend that at any given point, the decision needs to be made from the place where we find ourselves at that particular time and not with the imagined instincts of the person we want to become. This, too, requires a good deal of honesty and self-acceptance.

Building trust in ourselves and in our ability to make good decisions is something that continually develops over the course of a lifetime. It is normal to feel a lot of angst and weightiness around the bigger decisions in our lives, but the better we get at differentiating between fear motivators and trust, the more clarity we will develop in our thinking. If we internalize that the vast majority of our decisions are not between good and bad, or moral and immoral, then we can let go of a lot of the anxiety we feel around decisions and empower ourselves to be confident about the choices we make.

# PART II

# Decision-Making Case Scenarios

*Chapter 3*

# Introduction to Case Scenarios

Throughout our lives, we encounter many kinds of decisions. Some are significant and carry much weight, while others are far less consequential but still important. The following are case scenarios that relate to various types of decisions that may arise at different stages of life. The scenarios are meant to illustrate how the elements of decision making discussed in chapter 2 manifest and can be put into practice in a spectrum of realistic, everyday situations.

The specific details of each scenario are not what is important, and even the ultimate decisions that are presented are not meant to serve as recommendations for particular outcomes. The point is not to see ourselves in a description and to follow suit accordingly, but rather to recognize how the various elements of good decision making are either incorporated or ignored, and what can happen when fears are given room to dominate. The scenarios demonstrate how components of trust can be developed and employed throughout life and how self-awareness regarding trust and fear can influence the decisions that we make. There is no one right decision for everyone, or even for a given person. The conclusions we reach regarding what to do will always come down to how each of us processes a situation and arrives at an answer to the question, What do you really want?

The scenarios are arranged primarily in chronological order, with decisions typically encountered by young adults presented first. The later chapters then discuss situations that can arise in middle age and beyond. Some of the scenarios refer to onetime, monumental decisions, such as what career to pursue, whom to marry, or when to retire, while others relate to areas of our lives that we must constantly manage, such as our personal budgets, our relationships, and shifting emphases in our religious lives.

We may find that some of the scenarios hit close to home, and we can relate to them directly as current experiences or as situations we encountered at earlier stages of life. At other times, an individual scenario may not speak to us directly but might still help us articulate broader, underlying issues of trust and fear that can apply to similar circumstances.

In our younger years, the goal is to develop positive and healthy approaches to making good decisions that are based in trust. As life progresses, decisions often become more complex and multifaceted, and it can be more difficult to tease out what fears are at play. The consequences of a decision may have implications for a greater number of people and even more stark ramifications for ourselves. The scenarios presented here are not meant to simplify the process or minimize the complexity of the decision, but rather to show how the differentiation between trust and fear is always relevant and can be useful in various ways at many different stages.

Taken together, I hope these scenarios will demonstrate and sharpen the language of trust and fear, which can help reveal deep, intuitive feelings that we often sense but struggle to articulate.

## Chapter 4

# School Choices

**Miriam: "I Have No Clue What to Do"**

*Miriam, a senior in high school, was incredibly stressed about where to spend her year studying in Israel. She claimed that she had absolutely no idea where she wanted to go and did not know how she was going to decide between her two options. Three hours before the midnight response deadline, she asked if she could come to my house to speak about it. As we sat down on the couch, she exclaimed once again that she felt completely lost when it came to making this decision.*

*"I have no clue if I want to go to School X or School Y. I keep going back and forth between them and really don't know which one is right for me."*

*"Well, where do you want to go?" I asked, expecting her to reply that if she knew the answer to that question, she would not have needed to come talk.*

*Instead, without hesitation she responded, "I want to go to School X because I think the learning there is a better style for me."*

*"Great," I said, "so let me get my computer and you can register for School X."*

"But what if School Y has better students? Maybe I should go there," Miriam said nervously.

"OK. Do you want to go to School Y because it might have better students?"

"No," Miriam said. "I want to go to School X."

"OK, so let's sign up for School X."

"But what if the location of School Y is better?" she added.

"Do you want to go to School Y because of the location?" I asked.

"No," she said. "I think I want to go to School X."

With a smile I said, "Miriam, it sounds like you want to go to School X."

"Yes," she said, "I do! You're right! It's true! I do want to go to School X. I guess I just wasn't ready to admit it to myself. Thank you so much for your help and your insight." We both laughed as I pointed out that I had literally not done or said anything other than reflect back to her what she had expressed.

For a young woman who moments before had panicked that she had no idea how to make the right decision, Miriam seemed quite sure of what she wanted for herself. She clearly had known all along where she wanted to go but was afraid that she would be missing out on something by not going to School Y. While perhaps someone may have argued that School Y objectively has better students, better classes, or a better location, Miriam admittedly did not feel a real desire to go there. As soon as she stated her fears and was able to realize that, despite them, she still wanted to attend School X, the decision became obvious to her. She only had to be given license to trust her instincts so that she could feel confident about her choice.

Sometimes, though, the fears are not about the opportunities we will miss if we turn down one of our options. Rather, the fears concern the very choice we are leaning toward.

### Ephraim: Switching Schools

*Jeremy knew that his son Ephraim, a tenth-grade student, was unhappy in his high school. He did not find the learning environment to be a serious one or his peer group to be particularly admirable. Jeremy raised the possibility of switching schools, but a new school would involve a long commute, more taxing hours, plenty of work, and finding new friends. Just the thought of any of those things was terrifying for Ephraim. Jeremy reassured him that he could always choose to stay in his current school and make the best of it. He reminded his son that no one was pressuring him to make a decision that felt overwhelming or too scary for him. And yet, something in Ephraim told him that switching schools made the most sense. He knew that he was afraid of all the changes and had a hard time understanding what made him so confident that this is what he wanted. But he knew that he did. And so, with courage and full awareness of all the potential hardships, he decided to go for it.*

*Now that Ephraim had decided, Jeremy was nervous. What if the challenges would be too much? Was Ephraim up for the dramatic changes this switch would entail? Had he been wrong to suggest it? Ultimately though, Jeremy knew that he had to demonstrate trust in his son and let him make the switch.*

Ephraim went through with the change, and as expected, the challenges of the new school were not simple for him. Ephraim knew, however, that this is what he wanted for himself, and he understood why he ultimately chose this path. As a result, even though sometimes he would question himself, he never regretted his decision, and his father felt good about it too.

As we mentioned earlier, in many situations, the exercise of making a pros-and-cons list can be helpful in revealing what it is that we really want – not because the length of the respective lists is determinant, but because clarity in thinking often emerges from the process.

### Shoshana: "I Just Want to Stay for *Shana Bet!*"

*Shoshana was very much enjoying her gap year in Israel and began to think about staying for a second year. She felt that she had so much to gain from the institution that she was in and had only begun to take advantage of all that it had to offer. At the same time, she was uncertain, because a spot was waiting for her at a prestigious college that she had worked very hard in high school to secure. She was excited about the opportunity to study there and felt quite unsure about delaying her enrollment, especially since most of her close friends would be matriculating in the fall. Taking a piece of paper out of her desk, she folded it in half and began to compile two lists. On the left side of the paper, Shoshana listed all the reasons why she should go back for college that fall. The list went on and on. There was so much about the college experience that was beckoning her. It certainly felt like the more correct and responsible decision. On the right side, Shoshana wrote the reasons why she wanted to stay in Israel for another year. This list was only a third of the length of the parallel list. At that moment, a friend walked by, noticed the list on Shoshana's desk and remarked, "So, I guess you decided you are going back for college."*

*"No," said Shoshana with surprising certainty. "I just want to stay for shana bet!"*

Compiling a concrete list of the factors involved in our decision can allow us to gain trust in ourselves that we are truly considering all facets of a decision and not denying or ignoring any of the aspects or possible consequences. If, at that point, we realize what it is we want to do, we can have full confidence that it must be what we are genuinely seeking for ourselves.

*Chapter 5*

# Career Options

Focusing on the immediate next decision that needs to be made is helpful in allowing us to make one good choice at a time.

**Judah: The Right Insight at the Right Time**
*When my husband, Judah, was in medical school and feeling stressed about what course of training to pursue upon graduation, lots of experienced and successful doctors had advice for him. Each one had a good suggestion, yet none seemed to resonate with the lifestyle and balance that was important to Judah. We started to feel anxious about how we would move forward. Just when we needed it most, the most encouraging perspective came from a family friend, Dr. Susan Thalheim, who said, "At the moment that you need to make this decision, you will figure out what is right for you."*

*Her reassuring words have stayed with us at every point in life where a decision had to be made. In truth, there would have been no way for Judah to have known at that moment in time what he was interested in as a career path. A couple of years later, however, when another family friend, Dr. Leeber Cohen, raised the possibility of considering emergency medicine as a specialty, the time was right for seriously exploring and entertaining the idea.*

Until that moment, Judah had not known anything about emergency medicine and had never considered it as an option. By the time, however, that a final decision about residency needed to be made a couple of months later, he had done a lot of research into the field and had all the information necessary to make a knowledgeable and sound choice.

We must trust that we will have the tools to make good decisions at the time that we will need to make them. Our job is to ensure that we do not let our fears get in the way.

### Amy: Walking Away from a Dream

*Amy was excited to become a dentist. Already as a little girl, she had been fascinated by the equipment in her dentist's office and often imagined herself experimenting with the different instruments when she went for her appointments. In high school she worked hard and took AP Biology and Chemistry so that she would have a head start in college. When she began college, she was filled with anticipation that the fulfillment of her life's dream was drawing nearer. Suddenly, however, when she began her junior year, dating and marriage became a major topic of conversation among her friends. Many wondered aloud if it would be too taxing to balance a demanding career that required years of training with raising a family. Amy felt herself sharing these doubts as well and wasn't sure what to make of them. Of course, she wanted to find a life partner and have children, but did that have to come at the expense of her giving up her dream to pursue the career that she had long felt passionate about?*

*Eventually, Amy gave in to her fears and decided to pursue an alternate career that required less years of training. Nothing excited her about the profession, but she felt too scared to pursue dentistry. At the age of thirty, Amy was successful in her field but was disappointed that she was still single. Filled with resentment and frustration that she had not become a dentist as she had wanted to, she decided to leave her job and begin dental school.*

There is nothing wrong with considering and weighing our various fears regarding a decision. It is of utmost importance to think honestly about the possible outcomes of a decision and to consider if we are ready to deal with those consequences and embrace the decision that leads to them. If our concerns cause us to now prefer something else, then we should trust that our research has led us to a new conclusion. In Amy's case, however, her decision to abandon the study of dentistry was made from a place of fear.

As long as fear is not the main motivator, there is no right decision. Someone else in the exact same situation may find herself genuinely wanting to pursue another profession, given the new perspective she has developed based on her research and considerations; but that was not Amy.

## A Personal Story: Becoming a *Yoetzet Halacha*
*I was in eleventh grade when I first heard Rabbanit Chana Henkin, dean of Nishmat, a center for women's advanced Torah study located in Jerusalem, describe her dream for creating the Yoatzot Halacha (Women Consultants in Jewish Law) program. Even before the program existed, I already felt intrigued by the prospect of learning hilkhot nidda in depth with the eventual goal of helping couples keep the halakhot related to intimacy with greater adherence and accuracy and with more appreciation. Six years later, when the program had become a reality and I had the opportunity to participate, I was no less passionate about the role of a yoetzet halacha, but I was a lot more aware of the fact that it was considered controversial and was not accepted by many rabbinic figures. I knew that if I completed the course of study in Israel and returned as the second yoetzet halacha in North America, I would likely be opening myself to attack and criticism. My motives might be questioned, and I might be suspected of having an*

*agenda. These fears were based on observing the reactions to the first American yoetzet halacha.*

*And yet, I knew that there were rabbis who supported and backed the program, most notably Rabbi Aharon Lichtenstein, to whom my husband and I often turned for guidance. I did research; I thought and discussed, and I weighed the different considerations. Ultimately, with the support of my husband and parents, I decided to enroll, despite the consequences that would possibly result. Some of the hard and personally painful scenarios I had imagined did eventually play out when I began to work as a yoetzet halacha, but the fact that I was prepared for them yet still believed in and wanted to work in the field despite them gave me the strength I needed to forge ahead.*

Decisions made from a place of trust are empowering and sustaining and give us the ability to feel good and confident about them, even in the face of challenges. However, they depend on careful thinking, deep reflection, and a good deal of honesty, including confronting the question, "Am I ready to face all of the consequences, both anticipated and unforeseen, of this decision?" An affirmative answer, long before those challenges materialize, can be crucial to maintaining endurance over time.

### Leah: More Content Than She Realized

*Leah, an instructor of psychology, had been teaching AP psychology in a yeshiva high school for over ten years. She very much enjoyed the classes that she taught and the relationships that she formed there, but from time to time she would still wonder if she would be happier teaching older students who were more intellectual and ambitious about their studies. One day, Leah heard that there was a teaching position available in a respected college. For weeks, Leah deliberated about what to do. To others around her, it seemed obvious that this was just what she had been waiting for. Leah herself had always thought that she wanted to teach in a university. But as time went on, it became more and more clear that what was motivating her to think of switching jobs was the fear of passing up a great opportunity. Acknowledging this gave Leah clarity, and she ultimately realized that she wanted to stay where she was. No longer plagued with doubts about whether she would be more fulfilled elsewhere, Leah settled back into her current job with renewed feelings of contentment.*

This process was not an easy one for Leah. She had to rethink what her goals were, what brought her satisfaction, and even how she saw herself. Leah deliberated for many weeks about what to do. But ultimately, moments of deep self-awareness and honesty regarding factors that are motivating our considerations often give us the necessary clarity to feel confident about our decision making.

# Chapter 6

# Aliya

Careful listening to what we say and how we express our different options (or finding someone who can listen closely and reflect our words back to us) can sometimes give us the insight that we need into our own thinking:

*Over the course of one week, two seminary students approached me to talk about staying in Israel and making aliya. Each one seemed completely overwhelmed by the task of making the decision and felt that she lacked the tools and perspectives to know the right thing to do.*

### Sara: "I Am Going to Look So Stupid"
*Sitting down with Sara, I noticed how awful she looked.*

*"What's wrong?" I asked gently.*

*"Well," she said, "I think it's the right thing for me to make aliya, but I just want to be sure that I am making a good decision."*

*"Do you think it's a good decision?"*

*Without pausing, Sara began to rattle off a list of all the reasons why she thought so. "First of all, this is where we are supposed to* be. *This is where Jews belong, and, eventually, we are all going to end up here anyway.... And ever since Bnei Akiva in tenth grade, I have been telling everyone that I am making aliya right after high school, so at this point it's impossible to imagine not staying. And if I go back to America, I am worried that I could get stuck there because of a spouse or my family, and then I won't ever make it back here. So, in short, I think the right thing is definitely to stay."*

The more Sara spoke, the worse she sounded. Listening closely, I couldn't detect anything in her short speech that suggested that she in fact wanted to actually be in Israel, by herself, at this stage of her life.

"*I hear all that and it all makes a lot of sense,*" I said softly. "*But do you want to be here?*"

Tears began to roll down Sara's face as she silently shook her head no.

"*Sara, you don't have to make aliya right now if you don't really want to.*"

"*But I've been telling everyone since tenth grade that this is my plan. I'm going to look so stupid.*"

Both Sara and I knew that this was not a compelling reason to stay in Israel. I reassured Sara that all any of us can do at any given moment in time is make the best next decision that stands before us, that there can be many opportunities in life to consider aliya; and that it seemed pretty clear that she knew what she wanted for herself for the near future.

Sara's story portrays how easy it is to lose ourselves both in the fears of what others will think of us as well as in our own judgments and fears about ourselves. Worried that going back to America was not the right thing to do, Sara was quick to deny her own instinct that as a nineteen-year-old, single woman, she would thrive more at home with her family and attending an American college. She was also afraid that if she returned home, she would get stuck there and never fulfill her dream of making aliya.

It was unclear, though, if making aliya was indeed a sincere, current dream of Sara's, or at least as important to her as she professed. If it was important to her, then she should trust that she would work hard to actualize it over time. However, if it was an aspiration that she thought about in tenth grade but no longer wanted, at least for now, perhaps it was because she had new information about what it means to live in Israel as a young adult, speak Hebrew, and be far away from family. At sixteen, she had a dream. At nineteen, she was thinking about the reality, and, in doing so, she was scared to confront her true feelings.

While she could push herself to make aliya despite all her fears, doing so may lead to frustration or resentment. Aliya can be wonderful, but it is challenging. In order to succeed, it is important to feel confident that we have made a decision from a place of trust in ourselves that this is what we want.

### Rebecca: "Is It Crazy That I Want to Be in Israel?"

*A few days after speaking to Sara, Rebecca and I met to speak about the same type of aliya dilemma. Rebecca expressed all the apprehensions that are normal for a young woman her age considering staying in Israel. Being far from family and friends was at the top of the list, as well as concerns over what to study, missing out on the American college experience, living on her own, finding a spouse in Israel, and raising a family in a culture that was not native to her.*

*The conversation with Sara fresh on my mind, I said to Rebecca, "Given everything you just shared, do you want to go home to America?"*

*Without pausing, she exclaimed, "No. Is it totally crazy that despite all my concerns, I just want to be in Israel?"*

It's not crazy at all! Rebecca knew that all her fears were legitimate ones that she would have to struggle with if she decided to stay in Israel, but she also felt deep down that this was exactly what she wanted. In Israel she felt at home, alive, and connected in a way that she had never felt before. She knew that she wanted to wake up each day in Israel and that she wanted to build her home in the Jewish homeland. While she shuddered to think about permanently living so far away from her family, she also knew that they would all make the effort to stay in close touch. Convinced that this is what she wanted and ready to own her decision and navigate its consequences, she felt excited to move forward to the next steps.

In both of these aliya decisions, it was important for Sara and Rebecca to think about what would be the **best next decision** at that moment in time. Sara might be committed to aliya and would hopefully come back to Israel in the future, but it was clear that she was not ready and did not genuinely want to undertake the challenge at that point. Rebecca was sincerely concerned about how her future in Israel would play out. She worried that she would miss her family and have trouble finding her soul mate, but it was also obvious to her that for now she wanted to try to build a life in Israel. She was sure that the next decision she wanted to make was to stay. Making the best next decision helps move us forward to the place we want to be.

### A Personal Story: Making a "Smart" Aliya

*After my husband, Judah, decided to pursue a residency in emergency medicine, our plan was to make aliya immediately after he completed his three-year training. As he started his third year, we began the initial preparations for aliya. We filled out the aliya application, I informed my employer that I would be moving that summer, and we told our landlord that he should look for new tenants. About two months into our planning, however, everything shifted. One night I heard Judah speaking on the phone with a medical student who was thinking of a career in emergency medicine and who was also interested in aliya. Someone had directed him to Judah to talk through his decisions. From where I was sitting, I overheard Judah say to him, "Shayna and I believe in aliya, but we believe in making a smart and thought-through aliya."*

Something about the way Judah expressed himself stopped me in my tracks. "Are we making a smart aliya?" I asked him the minute he got off the phone. "Because if that is what we want, then maybe we should stay in America for one more year. That would allow you to get work experience as an attending physician and earn the money that could enable us to buy a house with a lower mortgage."

A difficult conversation followed, as both of us had been excited about the prospect of moving that coming summer. Judah, especially, had been looking forward to reenrolling in yeshiva in Israel, and the idea of another year of grueling work in an emergency department was not so appealing, to say the least.

We were also afraid that people would judge us and not trust our intention to make aliya. "Yeah, just one more year, sure..." they would say, and how would we be able to convince them, and more importantly ourselves, that they were wrong?

Over the next few days, it became increasingly clear that the best decision we could make was to stay. We did research, consulting with family and mentors in Israel, who were encouraging of our thinking. We knew in our hearts that staying a bit longer would make a big difference in our ability to start off our journey in Israel on the right foot. We also understood that three years earlier, when we had told everyone that we were making aliya right after residency, we had no concept of how much a house would cost in Israel or of how uneasy Judah would still feel as a doctor after finishing his initial training.

We also had long promised ourselves that we would always try our hardest to make the best decision we could at the time we had to make it. Possessing new information that we did not have three years earlier allowed us to trust ourselves that delaying our aliya for a year was the best decision we could make. After much soul-searching, we trusted ourselves that we still wanted to make aliya and that despite what anyone else thought or said, we did not have to feel afraid that we were giving up on our dream.

That night, we shifted course. Eventually, Judah worked (more than) full time as an attending physician for a year, which gained him much-needed work experience and financed a down payment on a house. We embarked on aliya the following summer. All these years later, we remain grateful that we were open to pursuing the best decision in the moment. It has had a significant impact on our lives to this day.

There are many families who consider aliya but ultimately realize that they want to stay where they are for a host of different reasons. It could be that they want to live close to parents and grandparents, pursue fulfilling career options that are not available in Israel, raise their children in neighborhoods and send them to schools that they feel are unique to the local Jewish community, or feel comfortable expressing themselves in their native language. There is no single, right answer to the aliya question; what is important is that any decision is undertaken with trust and honesty about our balancing of values and about which tradeoffs are worthwhile to us. The hope is that we can make a choice that aligns with what we want for ourselves and our families.

*Chapter 7*

# Use of Time

**Alex: Saturday Nights**

*Alex was spending his year after high school studying in a yeshiva in Israel. He found himself wasting a lot of time on his phone or hanging out with friends that he did not particularly enjoy being with. When he saw a flyer advertising a learning program on Saturday nights, he felt conflicted about whether to sign up and commit to attending. On the one hand, he did not feel good when he was not productive. On the other hand, after a week of intensive classes and learning, Saturday night was a time that he felt he wanted and needed to relax. In his heart he knew that leaving that time open was important to him, but since Alex did not trust himself to use it well, he decided to sign up for the program. He felt guilty that he was not interested in learning more and thought taking this plunge might help him. A few weeks later, however, Alex found himself hating the program and resentful that he had committed to it when it did not really appeal to him.*

Instead of not trusting himself, Alex could have thought carefully about an option for Saturday nights that would leave him feeling productive and that also interested and excited him.

Sometimes it can work to "force" ourselves to do something. But not in this case. Not when guilt and fear are the motivating factors.

If Alex had started the learning program because he aspired to use his time well and thought this program was a good investment, then it more likely would have been a success. Our emotions will often follow our actions: "The heart is drawn after the deed" (*Sefer HaḤinuch*, mitzva 16). But this is usually true only regarding something we choose from a positive place.

Alex, at most, "wanted to want" to be drawn to that kind of commitment or hoped that making a commitment would spontaneously spark what was missing for him. But there are no shortcuts to deep growth, and Alex wasn't necessarily honest with himself about that. He was absolutely right to aspire. However, he latched onto an idea not because of its positive value, but because of what he was trying to run away from. And that decision, made from a place of fear, did not last.

### David: Volunteering or Computer Programming?

*David, an Israeli high school senior, was unsure of how to spend his Monday afternoons. One option was to volunteer in a hospitality center near a local army base, giving out food and drinks to soldiers. The other option was to enroll in a high-level computer programming course that would be challenging and stimulating. The "right" decision seemed obvious. David felt as if there were no choice to even be made. How could he selfishly pursue his own self-advancement and fulfillment when he had the opportunity to contribute to others?*

If only life were so simple! If David is devoted to giving to others, maybe he can ultimately do so in a better way if he first invests further in his own education and grows more capable and talented. His contributions at that point could be much more significant. Of course, that doesn't mean his programming course should necessarily override the opportunity to volunteer. It does mean, however, that David ought to think carefully about his options and not prematurely dismiss either one as illegitimate.

In the choice between two objectively worthy goals, it is not obvious that the option that appears to have higher raw worth should always be prioritized. For example, in discussing whether a person can ever choose to spend time on activities besides Torah study, Rabbi Aharon Lichtenstein comments:

> Some feel that, inasmuch as "Torah is the best merchandise" (in the words of the Yiddish aphorism), why should anyone devote any time at all to anything but the "best merchandise"? In one sense, this notion seems eminently sensible. But do we really conduct ourselves in this way in all areas of life? If someone says he wants a piece of bread and butter, do we tell him, "Fool, why bread and butter? What's more important? Bread! So why put butter on the bread? Take two pieces of bread!" Of course not. But the question is, what is the butter and is there such a thing within this sphere? (*By His Light: Character and Values in the Service of God*, 209)

Rabbi Lichtenstein believes that pursuits that are inherently valuable and add meaning to our lives have objective validity. Choices between them, then, aren't clear and absolute, but will depend on the context.

Is David already engaged in a lot of *ḥesed*, or is it completely absent from his life right now? Is he interested in programming because he sees personal economic opportunity, or does it stem from awareness that computer skills are increasingly relevant to just about any complex project, including *tzedakot*? These are just some of the things that David might want to consider.

Frequently, in our quest for easy answers, we try to reduce a decision between "good and good" into one between "good and bad." How much easier is David's choice if there is really not a choice at all, but just a moral test! However, David stands to benefit from a more nuanced, honest look, at both the various options at hand as well as his own predilections. If he knows automatically and instinctively what he wants, if only because he sees this as an easy choice of altruism over egocentrism, that is fine. But if he has any ambivalence at all (as perhaps evidenced by the tension he himself acknowledges feeling), then a more deliberate decision-making process is likely to leave him with greater confidence in the conclusion he comes to.

*Chapter 8*

# Personal Finances

How we use our money involves innumerable decisions throughout our lifetimes. We are constantly making small decisions, e.g., "Do I want to bake a dessert for Shabbat or buy one from the bakery?" But these types of minor, daily decisions can sometimes touch on bigger, underlying questions of priorities and values:

*"What if a weekly bakery cake adds up to hundreds of dollars a year? Are we still OK with that within our overall budget?"*

*"Does the way we spend and allocate our money for various purchases reflect the things that are important and meaningful to us in life?"*

There are many practical questions that we might face regarding financial decisions:

*"Should I take a reasonable job offer that doesn't pay as much, or should I hold out and try to find a higher paying position, even though I can't guarantee that I will land one?"*

*"Should we buy a big purchase (a car, furniture, appliances) new or used? Does it make more sense to spend more but get something that might be better quality and last longer?"*

*"How minimalistic should we be in our day-to-day lives? How much effort should we put into analyzing what brands are cheaper so that we can lower our supermarket bill?"*

*"How much should we cut back on the small pleasures of life in order to save up for bigger and more significant expenses?"*

The urgency and intensity of some of these questions may ease over time, as capabilities change and the future doesn't seem quite as unknown. Still, at every stage of life, financial decisions should be made from a place of trust and not fear.

### Michael and Shira: Happy at Home

*Michael and Shira had always been responsible and conservative when it came to managing money. As a young couple, they had been careful to live within their means. They always thought cautiously about what they could afford and if a particular expense made sense and reflected their values. This approach helped them make deliberate and smart choices, but it did not stop them from making some big purchases. They were ready and willing to spend money when they felt good and proud about the specific decision at hand. As an example, during their early married years, they had decided to buy a car, even though many couples they knew relied on public transportation or rides from others. They realized that a car would allow them to see their families more often and to spend more time with each other and doing things that were important to them, as opposed to sitting through long commutes. They continued to similarly evaluate other expenditures as life progressed.*

*One year, a tough decision they encountered was whether they should sign up for a Passover program. Their salaries had significantly risen over the years, and, for the first time, they could comfortably afford to take their family of six away for the entire holiday. It was exciting for them that they had reached a place of greater financial stability, but they were still not certain that they wanted to go away.*

*Many of their friends had raved for years about the various programs they had been to and eagerly shared with them all of the benefits of going away for Passover. Michael and Shira, however, finally admitted to themselves that, despite the effort involved, they really looked forward to celebrating Passover at home each year. They loved the unique Seder they had with their children, while lounging comfortably on the couches in the living room; they enjoyed making matza pizza and other Passover favorites throughout the week; and even the daily trips were always a lot of fun. The more they thought about it, the more they realized how content they were at home. They decided that even though they were happy to have the financial flexibility to consider going away for Passover, it did not appeal to them.*

Shira and Michael made a personal decision about how to spend their money. They realized that decisions about money are not only about what we can and can't afford but also relate to what we prioritize in our lives and what we want for ourselves. In this case, they acknowledged that the reason they had even begun to consider a Passover program was that it felt strange to not seriously explore an option that had become so "normal" among their friends. Eventually, they realized that there was nothing strange about following their intuition to stay home. When they were able to be honest with themselves about how they were feeling, they suddenly knew what to do.

Sometimes, our decisions about money might also affect what others think of us. This can complicate our ability to rely on trust in our decision-making processes.

### Zev and Michelle: To Move or Not to Move?
*The Cohen family had lived for several years in a modest home that they had just barely been able to afford at the time of purchase. Room was tight, but it met their needs and served them well. Now that they*

*were middle-aged and had climbed the professional ladder in each of their respective careers, Zev and Michelle debated whether they should move to a larger home. While they could certainly afford to move and would benefit from the extra space that a new house would offer, they were worried that their friends would look at them differently once they moved. They were also concerned that their children, whom they had raised to be conscious of the value of money, could be affected by a move to a larger home. After much angst and many sleepless nights, they decided to trust their gut that moving would be the best decision for their family and that they would work hard to maintain their friendships and values.*

The Cohens moved and had no regrets. They were thrilled that they did not let their fears prevent them from doing what they felt would be the right decision for their family, and they trusted themselves that the factors driving them to move were legitimate ones that reflected their values. Even if they lived in a larger house that better suited their family's current needs, they knew that they would continue to be the same people they were with the same priorities and the same group of friends.

## Chapter 9

# Therapy

The decision for an individual or a couple to pursue therapy can be a heavy one. We might wonder what it means about us if we need to turn to someone else for help. Therapy might unfortunately also carry a stigma in certain communities. Additionally, it can cost a significant amount of money and is time consuming. All of these factors can involve an element of fear and dissuade someone from pursuing counseling, even when it could be beneficial.

**A Personal Story: Processing a Traumatic Event**
*On a snowy, wintery day, we were driving on the New Jersey Turnpike from Philadelphia to New York. My husband was at the wheel, and we had two young children in the back seat. Suddenly, our car hit an ice patch and spun 360 degrees, crossing multiple lanes of traffic. I will never forget that terrifying feeling of the car spinning. When we came to a halt, our car was facing forward next to the divider, miraculously having hit no one, and no one having hit us. But what we were hit by was the stark awareness of the fragility of life and how easily our entire*

*family could have been taken in an instant. In the years following that event, any time that my husband was at the wheel, I would feel physically tense. I knew that he had done nothing wrong to cause that incident, yet driving with him would often trigger memories of that snowy day. Friends encouraged me to get help, but I was resistant. I knew what was behind my reaction and why I felt the anxiety that I did. I could not understand how talking about it would move me forward.*

Looking back now on that time period in my life, I can appreciate that there were two fears that stopped me from pursuing therapy. The first was related to my self-perception: *"I am strong. I am self-aware. I am resilient. I often help other people deal with difficulties. I usually know what my needs are and how to move forward. What is wrong with me that I can't seem to manage this on my own? Why can't I just get over this by myself? Why am I turning it into a bigger deal than it has to be?"*

The other fear was that it would be a wasted investment. My life was hectic, and I did not have time available for therapy, including the travel time involved. We were also a young family with a tight budget, and this would be a big expense. *"What if I invest all this time and money, and nothing changes?"* The thought of all that potential waste almost stopped me from doing what I knew I needed – and wanted – to do. After much procrastination, I overcame these fears and got the help that was necessary to process what had happened and move on.

### Avi: Living with Anxiety

*Howie's son Avi had struggled with anxiety since he was little. There had been ups and downs in Avi's journey, but Howie was hopeful that things were about to take a turn for the better. They had finally secured an appointment with a highly recommended therapist, and Howie was counting on this. Avi, who was nineteen, felt less sure. Avi had been seeing one therapist for the last three years and felt entirely comfortable with him. The therapist really understood him, made him feel heard, and had been helpful to him in many ways. Avi had come to terms with his anxiety and had learned to live with it, despite occasional flare-ups here and there. Howie, though, seemed to be under the impression that there was a cure out there and that the right therapist would be able to "fix" Avi.*

*Avi saw how important it was to his father for him to meet this therapist. Simultaneously, it was also clear to him that his father's persistence was motivated by fear about Avi's situation. Avi, on the other hand, felt he was in control of his life and was much more at ease. He wanted to make sure that they made a good decision about his future treatment plan.*

*With the new therapist, Avi felt patronized and infantilized. "All his expertise is worth nothing if I don't like him and don't feel good about my time with him," Avi thought. When he shared with his father that he would continue with his long-term therapist, Howie was devastated. He wanted Avi to at least give the new therapist a second chance.*

*It was a new and scary experience for Avi to disregard his father's advice, but Avi held his ground. He knew what he wanted, and he knew what was good for him.*

Trusting our own instincts can be especially difficult when people we trust doubt our judgment. Sometimes, however, when we find ourselves feeling something strongly, despite the fact that those we respect do not agree or see it our way, that alone can be the greatest testament that what we are feeling is real and should be considered seriously.

# Chapter 10

# Religious Observance

$\mathrm{A}$ complex source of fear in the life of a religious individual can be one's relationship with God and His commandments. So many elements of fear can influence our decisions in this area. Fear of what others (including God) will think, fear of what our observance says about us, fear of punishment, fear that we are not authentic, and fear of falling short can all play roles in our thinking.

### Devora: "Minyan Girl"

*Devora appreciated davening with a minyan each morning. In her coed yeshiva high school, minyan had been an intrinsic part of each day, and she had discovered how much she enjoyed and benefited from participating in a communal prayer experience. After graduation, she wanted to continue this practice, but she knew it would be challenging to do so while attending a women's seminary in Israel. When she arrived, Devora was delighted to find out that there was a local minyan down the block from her school. She woke up early each morning to attend the minyan and returned in time for her first class.*

*Devora's friends could not get over her dedication and would com-ment and joke about it often. At some point, Devora began to doubt her own motivations. She worried that maybe she was going to minyan only because she felt proud to be known as the "minyan girl." Devora consid-ered stopping when she realized that maybe her attendance at minyan was not genuine. Before making a final decision, she decided to discuss it with a teacher.*

*"Do you want to go to minyan?" her teacher asked.*

*"Yes, I definitely do. I've been passionate about this since ninth grade," she said with a shy smile on her face.*

*"Do you think you are going only to impress people?"*

*After careful thought, Devora responded, "No, because I go even when I'm home or on my own and no one else is around to know."*

*Her teacher summed it up. "It sounds pretty clear to me that you want to go to minyan, and that you feel good about why you go. So why would you consider stopping?"*

Devora was surprised by how simple the decision now seemed to her. Moreover, it was hard for her to believe that she had let herself grow doubtful of her own intentions and motiva-tions when she knew that they came from a solid and pure place. She tried to internalize her teacher's advice that she should learn to trust herself more and feel good about her instincts.

Sometimes not trusting oneself can lead to a decision that can be detrimental in the long run, even if it seems to be a wise idea in the moment.

## Ariella: Hair Covering

*Ariella was engaged, and she was torn about how she wanted to cover her hair after her wedding. Her long, beautiful, thick, wavy, blond hair had always been a big part of her identity, and the thought of cover-ing it would bring tears to her eyes. She already knew that she was not going to enjoy this obligation. Ariella also assumed that it would be especially difficult for her given that her own mother, aunts, sister,* and sister-in-law did not cover their hair at all, and she would be the first one to do so in her family.

Having studied the relevant sources, Ariella knew that some rabbis hold that one may leave some hair showing. Ariella, though, was afraid to rely on these approaches, for if she started her married life displaying some of her hair, she feared that she could not trust herself and soon enough would begin exposing more. Due to this fear, Ariella decided that as upset as she might be, the best decision would be to cover all of her hair.

In the first few months after her wedding, Ariella struggled greatly with this obligation. It was most difficult for her when she was at school. She thought that other students were judging her and not fully accepting her as "normal" because of her hair covering. She would return home at the end of the day frustrated and upset. Ariella felt the psychological toll this obligation was taking on both her and her marriage. Eventually she decided to stop covering her hair altogether.

While she was much happier with how she looked, she now felt consumed by guilt. She had never imagined that she would end up in this place.

For many women, covering one's hair is a difficult, delicate issue. For Ariella, her decision to begin her marriage with a full head covering was rooted in fear. If she had been honest with herself about everything she was feeling, it might have been better for her to choose a more lenient halakhic option (perhaps in consultation with a patient and sensitive halakhic authority). She might have found a standard that she was ready to take responsibility for and could commit to for the long term. Instead, Ariella chose a practice that left her feeling awful and that ultimately resulted in a final outcome that she did not feel good about either.

To be sure, there might be more at play in Ariella's decision than just trust versus fear. She seems to harbor strong notions about her own self-image, and exploring them further, whether before or after her wedding, might affect her feelings and perspective so much that what she wants for herself evolves as well. Still, that possibility doesn't negate the need for healthy decision making at every point, and a choice out of fear cannot substitute for deep personal growth. For where Ariella was at, her decision grated against her own instincts, and the resultant friction eventually surfaced.

### Rafi and Noa: *Shemirat Negia*

*Rafi and Noa had been dating for eight months and were on the verge of engagement. Rafi had already gone with Noa to pick out a ring, and their parents had met and discussed possible wedding dates. But suddenly, after talking to his friend Meir, Rafi felt nervous. Meir had shared that he and his girlfriend of five months had stopped being shomer negia. Meir had taken it for granted that of course Rafi and Noa, who were further along in their relationship, were not shomer negia either. When Meir heard that this was not the case, he exclaimed, "But no one I know is shomer negia! Are you sure you are really attracted to her? I just don't think it's possible to be shomer negia if you are in a really serious and intimate relationship."*

*Meir's remarks continued to ring in Rafi's ears. "Is something off in our relationship?" he wondered. "Is something missing?" Were they really the only ones who had succeeded in being shomer negia throughout their months of dating?*

*Until his conversation with Meir, Rafi had felt proud of their halakhic observance. He knew that he was attracted to Noa, but together they thought deliberately about their interactions so that they could remain committed to the halakhic system. Halakha was so important to them, and their relationship with Hashem and their Judaism was a big part of the bond that they shared as well.*

*After a couple of days of stressing on his own, Rafi shared his concerns with Noa. Noa was not worried at all. "You know how much we love each other, how much chemistry there is between us, and how much we want to be together. We are shomer negia not because we are attracted to each other less than other people are, but perhaps because we are committed more. There is nothing wrong with our relationship. To the contrary, the fact that we are committed together to something greater than ourselves and our personal desires is a testimony to the incredibly strong bond that we share. I am not concerned in the slightest."*

Rafi hung up the phone confident that Noa was correct. He felt it deep inside and understood it to be true. He knew how much he wanted to marry Noa and be her husband, and he also knew how important *avodat Hashem* was in each of their lives. With some time and perspective, he was also able to understand how a halakhically observant person like Meir needed to convince himself that no one is actually *shomer negia* in order to lessen the tension that arose from his own decisions and actions.

Perhaps the most insidious fear of all is the gnawing doubt that we are spiritual charlatans, that neither our convictions nor our commitments are genuine.

### Malka: "I Just Don't Know If I Care Enough"

*It was Elul, and Rosh HaShana was a couple of weeks away. I had just finished giving a shiur on teshuva when Malka approached me and asked if we could speak for a few minutes.*

*Malka began talking hesitantly. It did not take long for the tears to start flowing.*

*"I'm just not sure that I am doing teshuva this year," she said softly. "Usually it is on my mind, and I am thinking actively about what middot I need to work on, what mitzvot I need to recommit to, and which people I need to apologize to. But this year, even though I am going through all the actions, I'm not really feeling it in my heart."*

*"What do you mean?" I asked.*

*"I just don't know if I care enough," she sobbed. "Maybe I'm just doing all these things because this is what I have been raised to do in*

*Elul, but not because I feel bad about my actions and really want to do teshuva." She paused and then added, "I just want to feel like I care."*

I stood there in shock. Here was a student sobbing about teshuva and wondering if she felt connected!

"Malka," I said gently, "look at you. You are crying hysterically about whether your teshuva is real and genuine. Do you think that people who don't care about Hashem at all and who don't think teshuva is important cry at the thought that maybe the teshuva they are doing is not good enough?"

Rabbi Joseph B. Soloveitchik tells the story of Anselm of Canterbury, a monk, philosopher, and theologian who held the office of archbishop of Canterbury in the Middle Ages. The story goes that he fasted and prayed for three days that God should reveal a rational proof for His existence. "The Danish philosopher Søren Kierkegaard ridiculed him, saying, 'You fool; does a baby in his father's arms need proofs or signs that the father exists? Does a person who feels the need to pray to God require a philosophical demonstration?'" Rabbi Soloveitchik continues, "In a whispered prayer to Him, man finds God" (*And from There You Shall Seek*, 16).

Out of doubt comes certainty; out of angst comes reassurance. When we call out to God, even when we are fearful or angry, our genuine faith is never more alive. When Malka began to cry about whether or not she cared about *teshuva*, it became blatantly clear that she did.

In an essay entitled "The Source of Faith Is Faith Itself," Rabbi Aharon Lichtenstein describes what faith entails.

> The greatest source of faith, however, has been the *Ribbono shel Olam* Himself.
>
> At the level of rational demonstration, this is, of course, patently circular.... Existentially, however, nothing has been more authentic than the encounter with

*Avinu Malkeinu*, the source and ground of all being. Nothing more sustaining, nothing more strengthening, nothing more vivifying.

The encounter, of course, has been varied. In part it has been channeled – primarily through *talmud Torah*, but also through *tefilla* and the performance of mitzvot; or, if you will, by the halakhic regimen in its totality. In part, it has been random moments of illumination while getting on a crowded bus or watching children play in a park at twilight. Obviously, it has also been greatly varied in intensity. In its totality, however, whatever the form and content, it has been the ultimate basis of spiritual life. (*Leaves of Faith*, vol. 2, 366)

Implicit in Rabbi Lichtenstein's description is not only trust in God, but also an ability to trust our instincts that our experiences with Him are real. Faith, in a sense, begins not with belief in God, but belief in ourselves that when we experience "random moments of illumination," we can trust that the inspiration we feel is authentic. We can appreciate that these mundane moments are deep and significant and accept them without becoming skeptical and cynical. We are not being ridiculous for believing and knowing. We can let go and trust in that momentary, piercing intuition that we have just encountered the Divine.

Moreover, the best *avodat Hashem* comes out of trust in our own capacity for spirituality and the authenticity of our religious experiences. Trust motivates us to reach higher, be better, and challenge ourselves further. With a sense of grounding and self-worth, even lurking religious doubt can be managed. Religious self-doubt, on the other hand, is uniformly demoralizing and destructive.

## Chapter 11

# Dating and Relationships

Dating can trigger much tension and anxiety around decision making. How do we decide if we should go out on another date or if we have seen enough? How do we ensure that we make good decisions that don't result in either ending a relationship prematurely or, alternatively, dragging it on pointlessly?

When I was dating, my mother shared with me a rule called "date till you hate." She told me that it is worth it to keep dating someone until you feel confident that you want to walk away (not literally hate) and are ready to do so without turning back. In many conversations with people who are dating, I have found this to be sound advice that helps lead to good decisions that one can stand behind even weeks or months later.

If we reflect upon my mother's four-word pearls of wisdom through the framework for decision making I laid out earlier, I think they share the same principles. An initial step toward a good decision is thorough **research**. One needs enough information to make an informed decision, as well as confidence that collecting more data will not change the outcome. But how long does that take in the context of any given relationship? The answer can be days, weeks, months, or even (less commonly) years! One might feel impatient, or frustrated, or fearful of wasting resources in the meantime, but there is no way to reach decisions that we can trust unless we have confidence in the data sets they are based upon. Moreover, another key component to good decisions is **honesty**. We can try to convince ourselves that we are ready to make a decision about a relationship, but if we are not, the price of self-delusion (including an erosion of trust in ourselves!) is very steep.

An additional element of good decision making is focusing upon the **best next decision**. In many cases, it means answering a single question: Do I want to go out on another date with this person, or am I ready to confidently walk away? It doesn't matter whether it is the second or twentieth date that is at stake; it is often the only practical question we need to address. In other words, unless we "hate" – we are certain that we do not want to be with this person long term – we should probably go on the next date. On the other hand, if we are feeling confident that we are not drawn either intellectually or emotionally to this person and are not interested in further dates, it is also OK to trust our instincts and move on.

But what if we just don't know? Time goes by, dates accumulate, money is spent, but we neither "hate" nor "love"? From my experience, this is one of the most common fears in dating: "No matter what I do or how much time passes, I feel like I will never reach clarity." This is a real, genuine fear, and there is no easy way to dismiss it. The only response, I think, is to reinforce our faith in our fundamental ability to make choices. Part of our faith in *behira hofshit*, free choice, is the belief that God empowers us to choose well and consistently grants each of us the necessary tools and insight to do so. Furthermore, this conviction is reinforced by all the decisions we have made in life until now – including many that, at some point, probably seemed overwhelming and unresolvable.

Ultimately, the only genuine response to **fear** is **trust**: trust in God that we are created in His image as autonomous, responsible beings; trust in Him that we will reach a place of clarity; and trust in ourselves to know when we have gotten there.

Now, let's see what all this means in practice:

### Dahlia and Yair: "I Don't Want to Like Him"

*Dahlia had always been attracted to the assertive, proactive type. She herself was known as an ambitious, driven, and strong woman, and she thought that it only made sense that she find a partner that was her "equal." The only problem was that every time she dated someone like this, it did not seem to go anywhere. When Yair was suggested to her, she deliberated over whether to date him. Yair had a reputation for being gentle, sweet, and soft-spoken – all wonderful traits, of course, but not the usual qualities that attracted Dahlia. By the third time his name came up, Dahlia felt that she ought to give it a chance.*

*When they started dating, Dahlia was struck by what an amazing listener Yair was, how well he understood her, and what a calming effect he had on her, especially when she was worked up. She knew from her earlier relationships not to take these things for granted; yet, at the same time, she would tell her best friend that "I don't want to like him. He is so not the type that I always pictured for myself."*

*Her best friend encouraged her to stay with it. "Don't be ridiculous. You are not going to marry anyone that you think isn't right for you. Either you will go out, get to know him more, and fall in love, or you will end it when you are ready."*

*With that in mind, Dahlia continued to date Yair, and several months later they were engaged. Dahlia never imagined that Yair's personality would be the perfect balance to hers. She could not be happier and more at ease than when she was with him.*

Dating can often be a process of self-discovery as much as an exercise in learning about others. Dahlia knew instinctively what personality types excited and attracted her, but she was surprised to realize that the one with which she could successfully build a deep, caring, sensitive, and loving partnership was of a different kind entirely. How did she figure this out? With a combination of openness, courage, patience, and listening calmly to her inner voice.

That Dahlia decided to marry Yair doesn't mean that her natural affinities disappeared entirely or that she eventually fell in love with every single aspect of his personality. It can feel funny to say so directly, but part of deciding whom to marry is deciding which flaws we are willing to live with, which things on "the list" we can compromise on, and which things we are OK giving up completely. No matter how well a relationship is going, we know that people are complex and that relationships are multifaceted. We can absolutely love, admire, and respect certain sides of a person while still finding other traits of theirs less fulfilling or appealing.

No one out there is perfect (including us!), and when we decide to commit to someone, we must do so knowing full well which things are not exactly the way we imagined or hoped they would be. Each of us is of course entitled to decide what we consider non-negotiable, but once those things are in place, the relevant questions become: "Can I live with this 'flaw'?" "Can I be happy and fulfilled without this 'plus'?"

### Avital and Moshe

*Avital had been dating Moshe for eight months, and their relationship was in a good place. Avital was pretty sure that Moshe was "the one," but there was clearly something that was bothering her.*

*"He's everything I always imagined. He's sensitive, intellectual, committed, fun…" Her voice trailed off.*

*"But what?" I asked.*

*"But I don't have the same kind of spiritual conversations with him that I do with my friends," Avital said.*

*"Well, isn't it great, then, that you have friends? Does Moshe have to fulfill every single need that you have? Isn't this why we have lots of*

*different kinds of relationships in our life? If you love him, respect him, trust him, and want to spend your life with him, then you also have to decide if you are ready to accept and embrace him completely, including the parts of him that you hoped would be different."*

Sometimes, confronting our disappointments and being honest with ourselves that we are willfully choosing to give up on something can enable us to move forward happily and without ongoing frustration. The reality is what it is, and we have chosen it anyway, with full knowledge and awareness. Instead of feeling annoyed every time we encounter our spouse's weaknesses or feeling shaken that "maybe I made a mistake," we can be empowered to own our decision and feel good about it. We married the whole person and are thrilled about "the package deal," despite the imperfections that are present in every relationship.

While overarching questions about what we want and what we can live with are crucial, they will often answer themselves over time, with sufficient patience and reflection. At any given point during a dating relationship, though, the immediate, practical question to ask ourselves is: "Do I want to go out again and get to know this person more, or do I have all the information I need to be certain that I do not want this and am ready to walk away?" As long as we feel that there is more we need to learn about the person and the relationship (and about ourselves) in order to make an informed decision, then we have reason to continue in it. We can trust that when we have the information we need, we will know what to do, even if it takes more time than we would have liked.

### Rena and Binyamin: When Something Feels Off

*Rena had been dating Binyamin for six months. She liked him a lot, but something was just not feeling right. On paper, Binyamin appeared to be the perfect match for her, but when they were together, she would get a nagging feeling that he wasn't sensitive enough in ways that were important to her. Sometimes he seemed a little too self-centered and caught up in his own interests to give her the attention that she needed. Before meeting Binyamin, though, it had been difficult for her to hit it off with any of the men she had dated, and the thought of breaking up and starting over from scratch made Rena sick to her stomach. "It's almost worth it to get engaged just so I don't have to ever go on another first date," she thought to herself.*

*But as hard as Rena tried to ignore her feelings, something wasn't clicking; on the other hand, she also wasn't ready to walk away. She kept telling herself that after six months she should know what the right decision was, and she promised herself that she would make up her mind over the next few days. When a few days passed and she still wasn't sure what to do, she decided to call one of her mentors. The mentor listened closely and patiently to Rena's description of her relationship and then remarked, "Who said you need to know after six months? Where did you come up with that number? Go out until you know what you want, one way or another."*

*Rena hung up the phone and took a deep breath. She had been given permission to trust herself and her instincts. It was OK that she didn't know yet. She would figure it out.*

After another month of dating, Rena felt confident that she wanted to end the relationship. Even the dread of having to start over with someone else did not leave her wanting to continue dating Binyamin. At that point, she knew and trusted what was right for her.

To her credit, Rena gave herself the time that she needed to figure out what she really wanted. While Binyamin was crushed, even he had to admit that Rena seemed to have clarity about their situation, and that helped each of them move on several weeks later.

Had Rena ended the relationship before that extra month had passed, she may not have had the same level of trust and confidence in her decision. This is what happened to Eitan.

**Eitan and Tamara: Breaking Up in a Panic**

*Eitan had been together with his girlfriend, Tamara, since they were sixteen and juniors in high school. Now twenty-three and a senior in college, Eitan began to have doubts as to whether he really wanted to marry her. "Perhaps I only think I want to marry her because we have been dating for so long and she is such a fixture in my life," he thought. He had never dated anyone else and wondered what that experience would be like. He loved Tamara, and she did bring out the best in him, but maybe he should be testing the waters and seeing what else was out there. It was May, and he knew that there would likely be some eligible women on the summer program he would be attending.*

*After a terrible night's sleep, Eitan woke up in a panic that they had been acting irresponsibly and must break up. When he shared his decision with Tamara later that day, she could not understand where it was coming from.*

*"Are you unhappy? Do you feel like something is missing? Is there something about me that you really don't like?" Tamara cried.*

*Eitan shook his head no to all her questions as tears filled his eyes. "I just feel like this is the right thing to do."*

*"But is this what you want?" Tamara asked in total shock.*

*"I don't know," said Eitan. "I'm so confused, but I think this is what we need to do," he repeated.*

As we might imagine, only a few weeks later, Eitan called Tamara back to say that he had made a terrible mistake. In a moment of extreme fear, he had impulsively decided that he could not trust himself and their relationship, and that he must end it. With fear as the motivator, and without a real reason for why he would want to be with someone else, it is not surprising that Eitan began to doubt the decision he had made. Good decision making, even regarding tough and painful decisions, should at the very least leave us feeling confident about the process. Tamara, who had felt sure about the relationship all along, was willing to get back together, and she and Eitan were able to work through the fears that had overwhelmed him.

Eitan panicked because he was overcome with anxiety that maybe their relationship was not as good as he thought it to be. It can be entirely normal, though, to feel nervous as we approach one of the – if not, THE – biggest decisions of our life. Even when we are feeling good overall about a relationship, the prospect of moving forward can be overwhelming during those moments when we are struck by the enormity of that possibility. Someone can feel anxious, faint, or even nauseous. Experiencing these sensations is not pleasant, but what happens next is most important.

If we can turn to our partner and share our feelings, if they can hear them and support us through them, if they are understanding and not threatened, if they can reassure us and calm us down, if we walk away from the conversation in a better place than where we started – then we have good indicators that the relationship is indeed strong and that there is effective communication. If the very person who is making us feel nervous is also the one to whom we turn to calm us down and help us regain composure, then we can probably feel at ease that we are in good hands.

Finally, fears of wasting time or making the wrong decision are not the only fears that can drive decisions regarding relationships. Take the following example.

**Yonatan and Shani: "I Don't Want to Hurt Her"**
*Yonatan and Shani were dating for a few months and had reached a crossroads. Yonatan was going to be traveling for the summer and was having trouble deciding if he wanted to keep up the relationship long distance. On the one hand, he knew that the fact that they would be apart was not a reason to end the relationship if he was happy. On the other hand, he wasn't sure that he was feeling fulfilled in the way he was hoping for.*

*When he thought about it more, he noticed that lately he had stopped looking forward to their phone conversations and that their dates were not too enjoyable either. Furthermore, he no longer felt the same motivation to invest in their relationship that he did early on. At times he wondered whether he was not making enough of an effort and whether continuing to work on their relationship could yield results. With further reflection, though, he realized that it was interest, rather than energy, that he was lacking. And yet he was having a hard time deciding to break up.*

*That night, he sat down with his mother at the kitchen table. His mother listened carefully to everything on his mind. "Tani," she said quietly, "it sounds like you are not really into this. What is stopping you from breaking up? It seems pretty clear that you want to, no?"*

*As Yonatan tried to explain to his mother what was preventing him from moving forward, he heard himself say, "You know, Shani has really not had an easy time dating. I don't think she is set up so often, and this was her first significant relationship. I know I'm not so happy, but the thought of hurting her is killing me, and maybe that's why I should keep going out for now."*

*No sooner had the words left his mouth than he realized how foolish they sounded.*

If Yonatan knew that he no longer wanted to be in this relationship, continuing to date Shani and lead her on would not protect her from pain. If anything, it might hurt her more. If he was confident that he did not want to be with her any longer, then the fear of hurting her should not deter him from ending the relationship, no matter how much heartbreak it would cause. This newfound clarity and confidence gave Yonatan the strength to end the relationship with as much dignity, respect, and sensitivity as he could.

## A Word about Working Hard on a Relationship

It is important to note that Yonatan explored for himself whether it was just the need to work on his relationship with Shani that was discouraging him; he understood that this factor on its own should not be a reason to end it. When things start to get somewhat tough as a relationship develops, sometimes we might think, "But *this* can't be what it is supposed to feel like; a relationship should not take *this* much work. At some point shouldn't things just flow, fall into place, run smoothly?" But there are always going to be differences that need to be worked through between two members of a couple.

Sometimes the differences are a clear result of the homes they grew up in – what they take for granted and what they expect based on what they are used to. Every couple encounters this somewhere along the way. Sometimes a difference is already clear and noticeable when a couple is dating; other times it may not come up until they are married. For example, a wife may expect her husband to take out the trash because that is what her father always did, while her husband may be frustrated that his wife is not taking out the garbage because that was the norm in his home. Neither of them had paid attention to this growing up, and not until they got married did they realize that they had ingrained assumptions and expectations that they were not consciously aware of.

Alternatively, while a couple is dating, they may already realize that one person is more expressive with their emotions, says "I love you" frequently, and comes from a home where there is a lot of physical affection, while the other person may have grown up in a house with plenty of love but where it is not expressed in those ways. This can create tension and frustration, as one feels deprived of the love language they are used to and the other feels smothered or overwhelmed by the constant mushiness.

One of the most important parts of any good relationship is strong communication – the ability to talk about things, address issues, and work things through. When a couple takes the time to identify issues and discuss them instead of denying or ignoring them – both during dating and later on – they can hopefully reach a better understanding of each other and of themselves and will more likely find workable solutions that satisfy both of them. Even years into marriage, a couple can continue to discover the ways in which their different upbringings and personalities impact their relationship. If they want their marriage to remain strong and fulfilling, it means taking the time to get to the root of the tensions and to discuss them openly.

The couple that snaps at each other over who takes out the garbage can make up, brush it off, and move on...until it happens again, or they can sit themselves down for a heart-to-heart talk on the couch about why this keeps happening and hopefully discover that their divergent expectations are what is driving the ways they are currently reacting. While conversations like these take time and energy and can be emotionally draining, they hopefully move the couple continually toward a deeper, closer, and more meaningful connection.

Sometimes, though, differences can be deeper. Two people can have different ways of reaching decisions, different instincts, different means of processing information and working things through, and different ideas with regard to how things should be done. One member of a couple may like to introspect on their own; the other may appreciate talking things out. One may like to consult with mentors when making a decision; the other may feel more confident deciding things by themselves. Since these differences are often connected to the very ways in which they communicate, they can be more difficult to process. Still, with a lot of self-awareness, openness, and concerted effort, these gaps can often be bridged.

However, if a couple feels that they have arrived at an impasse in working something through on their own but do not want to walk away from the relationship, it can perhaps be beneficial to consult a therapist. A professional might be able to help a couple understand each other better and learn to appreciate, accept, and work with the differences between them. If they are happy in the relationship but have hit some roadblocks, investing time and effort (and money) into exploring areas of tension can be worthwhile, especially since these issues are likely to continue to manifest themselves. Additionally, with certain realizations someone may also decide to see a therapist on their own, as an individual, if they think that could help them have a safe space to reflect, process, and understand the emotions and experiences they are having so that they can communicate better with the person they are dating.

When building a relationship, we are forming the foundation of communication skills that will, God willing, accompany us and serve us throughout our married lives. What we invest up front in developing this ability can go a very long way.

## Chapter 12

# Engagement

As a relationship becomes more serious, the looming decision to commit to someone for the rest of one's life can be extremely overwhelming for many people. Even those in the best and smoothest of relationships can begin to get nervous and experience doubts. The following scenarios have played themselves out over and over, in different variations, in conversations that I have had with many young people over the years:

**Dafna and Yaakov: "Maybe I'm Not in Love"**
*Dafna and Yaakov were on the verge of getting engaged when Dafna called, very nervous that maybe she was making a mistake. When I asked her to explain what was bothering her and if there was anything specific on her mind, she had trouble articulating any real concern.*

*"Do you trust him? Do you think he will be a good husband and father?"*

*"Absolutely; without a doubt," she replied.*

"*Do you respect him? Do you like his values? Do you enjoy spending time with him?*" There was not a single question I asked that Dafna did not respond to positively.

"*So, what is bothering you?*"

"*I guess I just don't know if I'm in love with him.*"

"*What does that mean?*" I probed. "*What do you think is missing?*"

*Dafna could not think of anything missing, especially since she was so happy and calm whenever she was with Yaakov. After a long pause she said, "Whenever I see Lauren, she looks like she's flying high and really in love with her fiancé. I don't know if I have that with Yaakov, and then I get scared that maybe something is wrong.*"

Dafna felt good about her relationship until she started to look over her shoulder, compare herself to others, and wonder if they had something that she did not. Little does Dafna know of all the challenges that Lauren has faced in her own relationship. We can never guess just from looking at people what is really going on in their lives. Dafna also has no clue of the image that she projects and doesn't know that just last week, her friend Rivka voiced concerns that maybe she is not as happy in her own relationship as Dafna seems in hers.

We do ourselves much harm when we look at others and begin to worry that something is missing in our lives. When Dafna was able to acknowledge the root of her fears, she realized how blessed she felt to be with Yaakov and how certain she was that she loved him and would be happy as his wife.

Help in figuring out what we really want sometimes comes, ironically, from having to face the alternative.

### Tova: Flipping a Coin

*After dating, breaking up, and then getting back together with her boyfriend more than once, Tova knew that she had to make a final decision to either get engaged or end their relationship for good. She deliberated intensely and gave herself a deadline by which she had to decide one way or the other. When she called to tell me she was engaged, I asked her, "So how did you decide in the end what to do?"*

*"I flipped a coin," she said without missing a beat.*

*"I don't believe you for a second," I responded. "Come on, tell me for real how you knew?"*

*"No," she said. "I really flipped a coin. I just had to flip it a few times until it landed on what I wanted!"*

Tova's story has stayed with me, and I have shared it many times with individuals struggling with tough decisions. While claiming she had no idea what to do and what she wanted, the minute the coin told Tova to break up, she felt herself instinctively resist. Somehow, she had known all along what she really wanted. All she had to do was to be willing to trust her instincts.

We need to trust ourselves in order to make a good decision. And when it comes to deciding whom to marry, we also need to trust a future spouse. It is hard to commit to someone without feeling deep trust in who that person is. This includes trust in their values and religious commitment, in the kind of spouse that person will be, and in how he or she will parent, support a family, and live life. We can never plan for every situation that may come our way, but if we develop respect for and trust in the other's thoughts, reactions, feelings, intuitions, behaviors, and way of processing events, then we will feel confident that whatever issue arises, we will be able to discuss it, navigate it, and work together toward making a reasonable decision that leaves us both feeling good.

### Esti and Shimon: Religiously Compatible?

*The longer Esti dated Shimon, the more she found herself respecting him and his opinions. When Shimon had originally been suggested to her, she had been nervous that they were not quite on the same page. Shimon had studied in a yeshiva whose hashkafa was known to be more to the right than Esti's was. Since a few different people had suggested that they meet each other, they agreed, curious to see what* everyone had in mind. As they got to know each other, they discovered that they pretty much agreed about everything that mattered. Shimon was considered open-minded for his peer group, while Esti was known to be on the more conservative side of her group of friends, and they seemed to meet in the middle on most issues.

As the relationship got more serious, however, Shimon began to ask Esti lots of practical questions that were bound to come up in the future. How did she plan on covering her hair? What kind of school did she imagine sending her children to? How would she dress when they were on vacation? Esti really liked Shimon and wanted to see this work out. She wondered to herself, though, how much she should be committing to Shimon's preferences just so that the relationship could move forward.

Relationships must be predicated on trust. Marriage can't unfold with an expectation that one spouse will change to fall in line with what the other wants. There must be a basic level of trust in who the other person is and the choices that he or she will make. Either Shimon trusts (or comes to trust) Esti's level of observance and approach to religious issues, or he doesn't.

Even if Esti gives him the "right" answers now and commits herself to them, there are bound to be lots of corollary questions that will arise over the course of a lifetime. It is hard to encourage Esti to move forward with someone who does not seem to trust her and her instincts.

A couple does not need to agree on every issue, but they should certainly be able to respect and understand each other's perspective. They need to feel trust in the other person's values and how they will manifest in different situations. As Shimon continued to date Esti, he did develop this trust in her, and Esti ultimately felt appreciated for who she was.

**Post-Engagement**
Even after a couple decides to get engaged, the process of getting to know and trust each other and of interacting more naturally

and comfortably with one another is still ongoing. Just because a couple feels ready to get engaged does not mean that they immediately feel ready to be married – to live together, share a bathroom, or be intimate. As long as they trust that slowly, they will get there, this does not have to be a cause for concern. So much growing as a couple happens between the day they decide to get married and when they stand under the *ḥuppa*. It is natural to discover during engagement that we are still in the middle of that process. Two stories from my own engagement frequently come to mind when I think about this point.

## A Personal Story: The Pinball Game

*One Saturday night, a few months into our engagement, Judah and I were hanging out in his apartment. We were in a relaxed and fun mood, and we began playing a pinball game on the computer. It was a simple game that didn't require too much skill or strategy, but it still got intense and competitive, and also quite silly. I remember Judah turning to me, smiling, and saying, "Wow, I have never seen you like this. I don't think I really knew about this side of you!" And it was true. Though we had dated for five months and were already engaged for a few more, I was aware that he had not seen those parts of me that only came out late at night with my sisters or roommates when we were in pajamas and a little hyper.*

*This hadn't worried me, though, because I knew that while our relationship was solid and deep, we had not yet hung out in those ways. I felt confident enough at the time of our engagement that in due time that side of me would come out, when it got late enough and I was overtired and disinhibited. I knew Judah would accept that part of me (and even be amused by it!) and that I would feel comfortable with him. Therefore, it didn't bother me that it had not happened yet. I was OK with that, and that is what was crucial for me.*

*There were other feelings and experiences, however, that I knew I needed to have before I could get engaged. It was important to me,* for example, that we spent a few Shabbatot with each of our families before we decided to get married. Every person has to figure out what those things are going to be for themselves. For me, though, being silly happened to not be one of them.

## And One More: The Speeding Ticket

*Ten days before we got married, I was driving from the Catskills to Judah's house so that we could spend some time together before we parted for the week leading up to our wedding. I was anxious to see him, and I was aware that I was driving over the speed limit as I made my way down Route 17 in Upstate New York. Only when I was pulled over by a police officer, however, did I realize just how fast I had been driving. He handed me a ticket with a high fine and several points on my license, and he scolded me harshly for far exceeding the speed limit. As he pulled away, I broke down in tears, sitting in my car on the side of the highway. I knew I had been irresponsible, and I felt awful about the ticket I had just received. Immediately, I called my father, crying hysterically about what had happened and how terrible I felt.*

*Only after he consoled me and I hung up the phone did it strike me that at the age of twenty-three and ten days away from getting married, I had called my father and not my fiancé. While I definitely took note of this and wondered if it was strange, I also intuitively knew that things would naturally evolve over time. For so long I had called my father to be a calming voice whenever I was worked up and, once I started to drive, to help me with car issues. It made total sense that I instinctively turned to him when something went wrong. I knew, though, that once married, when driving our own car, with our own insurance, and living day-to-day life with Judah in our own home, I would turn to him if I were ever pulled over by a police officer again (as indeed has happened a couple more times… ). That knowledge allowed me to feel comfortable that it was just a matter of time and that it was OK to embrace that process without feeling unsettled that something was wrong.*

## It All Comes Back to Trust

In order to feel confident that we have the kind of relationship that will continue to grow and develop over the course of a lifetime, we need to feel tremendous trust in the other person – trust in their ability to communicate, to understand us, to be there for us, to respond in the ways that we need, and to help us move forward. We also want to trust in their values; in their priorities; in their interactions; in their religious observance; in the kind of parent they will be; in their financial responsibility; and in the way they carry themselves and handle frustration, anger, and other difficult emotions. There are no shortcuts to developing this trust. Rather, it accumulates over time by observing someone and spending time with them in a multitude of situations and in various venues.

The passage of time can also be very helpful because it inevitably brings both a loosening of inhibitions as well as a variety of experiences that expose us to more sides of a person. Seeing how they act and react in a wide range of environments and circumstances and with all kinds of people can be the greatest reassurance of who they are at their core, and, in turn, this enables us to establish the trust that we need in order to commit to building a life together. Every couple should feel comfortable giving themselves the time they need to feel ready to take this step and should not succumb to external or internal pressures pushing them to make a decision before they are ready to.

When a couple feels deep trust in and respect for one another and has good communication between them, they will hopefully be able to navigate anything that comes their way. To trust another person, however, we first need to learn to trust ourselves and our intuitions. We need to learn to listen to our inner voice, to make decisions from a place of trust instead of from fear, and to think about what we really want. The ability to trust ourselves is ultimately what empowers us to be able to make good decisions, own them, and take responsibility for them moving forward – never more so than regarding the decision of whom to place our trust in and marry.

*Chapter 13*

# Having Children

Having a child is an irreversible decision. It is perhaps one of the only ones in life that cannot be undone or reassessed. This is likely one of the reasons why people consider the question of having another child very carefully, and fears in this area can be quite daunting.

**Jennifer and Adam: Baby Number Six?**

*Jennifer and Adam had five beautiful children. Although Jennifer could sometimes feel overwhelmed with managing all their needs, she loved each child deeply and was so content and fulfilled as a mother. Jennifer herself had grown up in a family of five children and had always imagined the same for herself. Once she had given birth to her fifth, she could not help thinking that her family was complete.*

*Now that their youngest was three, however, and day-to-day life had somewhat calmed down, Adam began to raise the idea of having another child. Jennifer was surprised, even taken aback. The thought* had never even crossed her mind, especially since five children was already considered a large family in the community in which they lived.

Jennifer felt nervous about the idea. Six kids sounded like too many. What would people think of them? Would they be able to support another child? Would she have the energy and love that was necessary to raise an additional child? Filled with fears, Jennifer told Adam that she was not sure that she could handle another baby. "Just think about it," Adam said to her, and left it at that.

Over the next few weeks, Jennifer was so busy with work and homelife that she did not have any time to think seriously about Adam's suggestion. Suddenly, though, she began noticing every infant she passed. She found herself watching babies, and especially the mothers holding them. The longing for another child began to well up inside of her until she was sure it was what she wanted. Letting go of her fears and hesitations, she knew that they would make it work.

Being honest with and deeply attuned to ourselves is critical to strong decision making. If we feel overly tied to our previous assumptions, we won't allow ourselves to pursue new dreams and goals. While there is no need to force ourselves into something that we are not interested in, giving ourselves the room to think outside of our comfort zones can open horizons that we never anticipated. And, yet again, time can make all the difference.

# Chapter 14

# Divorce

The decision to divorce is one of the most difficult and painful decisions that a couple may face. How can one or both spouses know if it is right for them or not when there are so many factors to be considered?

**Chaim and Talia: Facing the Unknown**

*Chaim had been married to Talia for twenty years. They had four children, and on the outside appeared to be the perfect couple. When they hosted other families at their Shabbat table, there was always interesting conversation and a good dynamic. That is why Chaim was having trouble even entertaining the thought of getting divorced. People would be shocked and would not be able to understand it at all.*

*But they did not live in his house. They did not know how intense it was to live alongside someone who had manic-depressive tendencies. When Talia took her medication consistently and was in a balanced mood, she was a wonderful wife and a caring, energetic, and giving mother. That's how the outside world usually got to see her. But often, either she was down, or she was impulsive, angry, and frankly out of control. When Talia was feeling depressed, she became completely intro-verted and absorbed in her own issues and was not able to see beyond and outside of herself. That was not as bad, though, as her swings to the opposite pole, which could make her nearly abusive toward Chaim, and sometimes toward their children.*

*Chaim had a lot of compassion. He loved Talia deeply, just as when they had met, and he really felt for her. He knew that she had not been given an easy lot in life. But he at least needed her to continue her therapies and be committed to taking her medications, as they had discussed she would when they had dated. When she did not, there was total havoc in the house.*

*For years, every time Chaim considered divorce, he would worry about how it would affect the kids and if he would be able to manage on his own. Lately, though, he had begun to think more about how perpetuating this marriage was impacting his kids. "Perhaps a divorce would be better for them than continuing to witness this dysfunctional relationship," he wondered.*

*At some point Chaim found himself imagining his oldest daugh-ter's wedding several years down the line. He envisioned being there as a single, divorced father, while Talia glowed with a new husband. Though the fear of being alone, and lonely, was real, nothing seemed to be as tough for him as the thought of staying with Talia. Chaim felt deep sorrow for where things had come to, but he knew that he wanted to end his marriage and advance to a healthier place. After months and years of agonizing about the decision, he finally had clarity about what he wanted to do.*

On the virtual pros-and-cons sheet in Chaim's head, the "con" list for divorce was long and intimidating. But when Chaim real-ized that what was keeping him in the marriage were all of his fears – fear of what others would think, fear of the effect on his kids, and fear of loneliness – he was better able to weigh if he wanted to stay because of those reasons. This didn't make his situation any less complicated, but it did cast his decision in a new light. Realizing that he could face those fears is what freed him to make the decision he felt was best for him and his children.

## Eli and Adina: Doubting Doubts

*Eli and Adina had gotten married on the later side, and sometimes Adina wondered if she had only married Eli out of fear that she would be alone forever. They were six months into marriage, and thoughts would creep into her head: "If only I had dated the next guy, things could have been different."*

*It wasn't that she didn't like Eli, but he was so different from what she had always imagined. He was louder than most of the men she had dated. He was passionate and funny, but sometimes his humor could be unintentionally offensive. He wore his emotions on his sleeve, and sometimes when they were in public she felt embarrassed that he came across as undignified.*

*Adina became obsessed with the thought that perhaps she could have done better. She wondered if maybe she should get divorced now, before there were children and everything became a lot more complicated.*

*Often, though, just when she would lean toward divorce, they would have a nice experience together, maybe on an outing or at dinner. Adina would be reminded of all of Eli's wonderful qualities, and she would begin to doubt her doubts. Perhaps they were all just in her head. Or were they real? Sometimes she felt as if her brain were getting tied up like a pretzel.*

*In conversation with her close friend Julia, Adina hesitantly shared some of her worries. Julia explained to her that it can be normal to have doubts and that she did not need to make too much of them. Julia further told her that she could give herself permission to be happy and to enjoy her marriage as it was. If the doubts were real, they would declare themselves.*

*Finally, Julia told Adina to trust herself as well as the decision that she had made to marry Eli. "You make good decisions," she* reminded her. "There is a reason you married him. You dated tons of guys. You didn't just settle; you chose Eli. Now go and invest in your marriage."

Adina hung up with newfound confidence. She *was* happy. She could trust herself. And if something changed down the line, she could always reevaluate. For now though, all was good.

Would their marriage work? Only time would tell. At least Adina knew what her **best next decision** was. But in order to trust her decision, she first needed to trust herself.

*Chapter 15*

# Adult Children

A̲s children grow into full-fledged adults, with thoughts, opinions, careers, and even families of their own, parents are often confronted with difficult decisions regarding how to interact with their adult children.

### Shalom and Michal: Evolving Relationships

*Shalom and Michal were loving parents who had raised their four children with lots of care. Family dinners, vacations, long Shabbat afternoon board games, and lots of personal attention were all standard in their home. They had worked hard to instill their values and beliefs from a place of love and respect, and they felt proud of the parents they were and the close relationships they had developed with each of their children. After their first two children had followed closely in their path, it came as a real shock to them when their third child, Yishai, began to stray from religious observance in his early twenties. Over the following years, his commitment fluctuated back and forth, and they remained hopeful that he would eventually settle down into a life of traditional practice. But when Yishai introduced them to Tal, the young woman he planned on marrying, it became crystal clear that did he not envision a religious lifestyle for himself at all.*

*Beginning with the engagement, Shalom and Michal had to navigate the ins and outs of how they would interact with the new couple. One of the tougher decisions they faced was whether they would allow Yishai and Tal to come and go as they pleased over Shabbat. In their Israeli yishuv, there were other couples who faced similar dilemmas with their own adult children, and everyone handled it differently. While it was important to Shalom and Michal, and to their other children, that Yishai continue to be an integral part of the family, it was hard for Shalom and Michal to imagine their child and his spouse driving to the yishuv on Shabbat, parking outside the closed gate, and joining them just for lunch. What would their friends and neighbors (not to mention their rabbi) think about their parenting? Were they too weak to take a stand and uphold the standards of their home?*

*At the same time, they also feared losing their connection to Yishai and spent a lot of time deliberating what to do. They knew that whatever decision they came to, they had to be ready to take responsibility for it and to own whatever consequences it would bring. It took them a long time to determine what they really wanted, but, ultimately, they decided that they wanted Yishai and Tal to be able to join them, as long as their children committed to keeping Shabbat within their house.*

Even once Shalom and Michal came to this realization, they knew that there was still much that would have to be explored, talked though, and negotiated with Yishai and Tal. There were many underlying feelings that needed to be addressed, and they were also well aware that their perspectives on the issue could, and likely would, shift over time. Although for now they had decided to let the couple visit them on Shabbat, Shalom and Michal were also open with Yishai that the decision was not an immutable one and that their feelings might continue to evolve.

Sometimes the option of uncompromisingly upholding their values and their standards resonated with them deeply. They respected their friends who had chosen that path and wondered if, at some point, they would choose it as well. They knew that this discussion, and the decisions it required, would likely continue throughout their lives. And yet, for now, all they could do was make the best next decision. They were ready to take ownership of their choice as something they realized they wanted, despite the underlying complexity, rawness, pain, and sensitivity of the entire situation.

### Ari and Susan: Keeping Quiet

*Ari and Susan were a high-powered couple that enjoyed stimulating, intellectual conversations and spent hours sitting at their Shabbat table discussing and debating Torah, philosophy, science, politics, and literature. Their children enjoyed the conversations as well, and Ari and Susan took delight in the fact that they had raised thinkers who were well read and up-to-date on current events and other major areas of interest in the world. Ari and Susan were also incredibly satisfied that all of their children had pursued professional careers, married intelligent and accomplished people, and seemed to enjoy marriage relationships similar to their own. As their grandchildren grew older, however, things began to get more complicated.*

*Naomi, their oldest granddaughter, was talented and charming but had never taken a liking to school. She was quite capable, but school did not appeal to her, and she was unwilling to put the effort into her classes that was required in order to excel. She had managed to get by in high school, working just hard enough to pass, but she was completely unfazed by her poor grades, which frustrated her parents* and grandparents. After taking a gap year in Israel, Naomi returned home and told her parents that she did not plan on attending college. Instead, she would take a few business courses and pursue her dream of opening a high-end nanny service for wealthy families. Naomi had always loved children, had enjoyed working as a nanny herself a few times, and possessed great business sense.

When Ari and Susan got wind of Naomi's plans, they were disappointed and confused. How could their middle-aged children be so irresponsible as to allow Naomi to not pursue a college degree? What kind of adults and parents had their grown children turned out to be? How would this look to Ari and Susan's own friends and community? And how could Naomi be so foolish as to think that this was a life plan?

In conversation with Ari and Susan, Naomi's parents didn't sound thrilled either. But they pointed out that they had always told her that once she finished high school, she was free to figure out what she wanted for herself. They believed in her street smarts and capabilities and were confident that she would be successful in life.

This conversation, however, only further exacerbated Ari and Susan's worries, as it began to sink in that they and their children were not at all on the same page. They now realized, though, that, as grandparents, they had to figure out how to respond. They were honest and self-aware enough to realize the many fears that were part of their concerns. Some of the fears they felt were legitimate, as they worried about Naomi's future and how she would support herself; they also knew, though, that some of their concerns were wrapped up both with their own self-image and with how others would judge them and their family. Ari and Susan understood that before they proceeded further, they needed to think long and hard about what they really wanted to do and how they wanted to interact with their adult children and grandchildren.

Even those who have passed most of their own major decision-making crossroads in life can still be roiled by the decisions of others. In some ways, these dilemmas can be even harder to deal with, as we have far less control. Furthermore, the more a family grows, the greater chances are that there will be outliers who go off on their own paths. Ari and Susan need to think carefully about what their role is in this situation and what it is that they really want as they decide how to respond.

*Chapter 16*

# Retirement

The decision about when to retire can naturally be fraught with uncertainty and anxiety at an upcoming major transition. Therefore, as always, it seems crucial that these decisions stem from trust.

**Jerry: Corona Curveball**
*Jerry had practiced dentistry for forty-seven years. He had worked hard to build up a large and successful practice, with lots of loyal patients who had been coming to him for decades. Jerry enjoyed his work, was an expert at what he did, and was invested in the relationships that he had developed with his clients. Before the coronavirus pandemic erupted in 2020, Jerry had been expecting to work for at least another three years. His hands were still steady, he felt confident in his abilities, and going to his office every day gave him a sense of purpose and fulfillment.*

*But after the virus hit, everything changed. Suddenly, dentistry became the most dangerous profession, since it required hours of work in patients' open mouths. Even the best mask could not guarantee full* protection. In his mid-seventies and on medications for high blood pressure and diabetes, Jerry knew that he was in a high-risk category. At the moment, so much was unknown about the future. Jerry imagined that even if the pandemic eventually passed and life slowly returned to normal, he might still worry about whether his clients were carrying the virus and could endanger him without even realizing it.

Before the virus had changed day-to-day life, Jerry had been terrified of retirement. He was afraid of being bored and restless and concerned that being home full time might negatively affect his marriage. He loved his wife dearly but also knew that the time they spent apart each day and the space that they gave each other were good for their relationship.

Over the couple of months, however, during which Jerry and his wife, a practicing attorney, were sheltering at home, Jerry found himself really enjoying his respite from work. He had more time to speak to his children and grandchildren, develop his cooking skills, exercise, and invest in his various hobbies. When his wife was not busy working remotely, they had begun playing card games, working on crossword puzzles together, listening to shiurim, going for long walks, and thoroughly enjoying each other's company.

For the first time, Jerry found himself seriously considering retirement. Financially, they were secure, and he could retire now without worrying about the future. At the same time, Jerry would then stop himself and think: "Do I want to retire now only because I am worried about my health? Am I secretly concerned that my practice is going to fall apart and that my clients will not return?"

These worries bothered Jerry. He did not want to make a decision that he would regret in the long term. He knew that he should give himself the time he needed to feel secure with his choice. Over a few months' time, it became more and more clear to Jerry that despite what he had always believed, he was actually excited about retirement and was ready to bring his successful career to a close and begin the next stage of his life. He felt good about his decision and began to move forward with the legwork that needed to be done to sell his practice.

Sometimes it can be confusing to determine whether trust or fear is motivating a decision. Jerry gave himself the time he needed to be sure that his decision was coming from a place of trust and not fear. He felt unclear regarding whether he really wanted to retire or was considering it now only because he was afraid of what would become of his practice. On the other hand, when he thought about continuing to work, he was unsure if that desire was motivated by his love of the profession or, alternatively, by his fears of facing the unknown future that retirement would bring with it. Over time, it became easier for Jerry to sort it all out. When he had clarity about what he really wanted, he knew that he was ready to retire.

## Debbie: Not Done Yet

*Debbie had been working as a tour guide for many years. Over that time, she had developed a stellar reputation and was sought out by many families, groups, and organizations who visited Israel. She took her work very seriously and always came prepared and well read on whatever area of the country they were touring. She had a wealth of knowledge and information and was always ready and able to answer any question that her clients asked. On occasion, if Debbie did not know how to respond to a specific inquiry, she would follow up and get back to the questioner, even if their time together had already ended. She was thorough and dedicated and genuinely loved her work.*

*Lately, though, Debbie had been feeling that perhaps the time had come to retire. She understood that she was not as flashy and energetic as some of the younger guides. She was not as creative and exciting and felt that she could not compete with the thrills and frills that they offered. In her heart, she realized that she knew more than they did and was far more experienced, but she worried that over time, the younger generation would gravitate away from her, and she would end her career on a low. With a heavy heart, she decided to close her business and retire from guiding before that would happen.*

Nothing about Debbie's decision came from a place of wanting to retire. It was all based in fear. Not surprisingly, as time passed, she found herself questioning her decision and doubting whether it had been a wise one. After a few past clients expressed real disappointment, Debbie decided to go back to work and continue guiding, as long as clients were interested in her services and she was up for the task.

No matter what situation or scenario we find ourselves facing over the course of our lives, it can always be beneficial to ensure that our decisions emerge from a place of trust and not fear. That will allow us to feel good about, take ownership of, and stand behind our choices and their consequences.

# PART III

# Employing Trust in Everyday Living

*Chapter 17*

# Raising Children with Trust

The dichotomy between trust and fear might be felt most sharply in moments of decision making, but these two elements form an axis that exists in every area of our lives and is not limited only to situations in which we face a stark choice. Whether we operate out of fear or out of trust influences the attitude we bring to life's everyday challenges and our interactions with the diverse figures in our lives, such as friends, colleagues, and spouses. Furthermore, relationships frequently present us with the opportunity to support others' trust in themselves. And while this can be true even for adult peers, it is particularly crucial for our youth, who are actively developing their characters and personalities.

In the realm of education, I believe that we can raise our children on principles of trust and that, as parents, we can navigate the challenges of this process with trust rather than fear. While this book does not intend to present a comprehensive approach to raising children, I do want to discuss some common manifestations of trust and fear that arise in the context of parenting.

My personal role models for parenting with trust are my own parents, who spent forty-five years as the rabbi and rebbetzin of a Modern Orthodox synagogue in New York. My sisters and I grew up as "the rabbi's daughters" in a community with diverse approaches and commitments to Judaism and with people whose observance level was often quite different from the standard in our own home. Nevertheless, it was important to my parents that their children did not become suspicious or fearful of those around them.

I am sure that my parents were nervous about some of the influences that surrounded us growing up. Under the circumstances, it would have been much easier for them to forbid us from attending certain bar mitzvas or from going to certain houses altogether than it was to consistently explain their expectations for us and affirm their trust that we would rise to each challenge.

They worked hard to imbue us with the halakhic values and practices that were so meaningful to them while also teaching us to trust the world in general and the people of our community in particular. They strove to speak and act in ways that did not cause us to look down on the standards of other families. While teaching us to be proud of our own commitments and lifestyle, they also emphasized the *tzedaka, ḥesed, middot,* and *mesirut nefesh* for Judaism that stood out in the lives of others.

My parents didn't necessarily speak in terms of trust versus fear, but when I happened upon that language later on in life, I realized how well it described that which was most familiar to me. Like any parents (or perhaps even more so), my mother and father could harbor anxieties about our well-being, but when it came to our choices and our overall trajectories, they exuded trust and encouraged us to trust ourselves and our instincts. So often, when I felt stuck, it was one of my parents who helped me see that

I would find my own way forward. And on one occasion, when I was plagued with self-doubt after a misguided decision that went sour on me, it was my mother who persistently reassured me that I would have eventually reevaluated and changed course on my own.

### EMPHASIZING POSITIVE MOTIVATORS OF BEHAVIOR

As I got older, I appreciated that my upbringing, based on trust, was not something to be taken for granted. In raising children, it can certainly be tempting to turn to fear of "the outside world" and fear of "the other" as powerful motivators of behavior. It is not difficult to scare a child into thinking that everything different from or foreign to his home is threatening and, in this way, to push the child to do what is wanted of him. But what happens when the child is no longer afraid? What happens when she is on her own and needs to make her own decisions? What happens if, or when, resentment sets in? Educating out of fear works very well – for the short-term. But if we, as parents and educators, are seeking long-term results, then we should want our children and students to develop trust in their own values and confidence in their abilities to make good decisions, even when there is no fear involved.

Similarly, in raising young, religious children, we need to nurture positive feelings toward our religious values and practices rather than wield the intensity of fear as a tool. Shabbat, for example, is a wonderful experience that should be associated with uplifting feelings and activities. It should be permeated with entrancing sounds and smells, tastes and images, rather than with parental angst or harsh scolding in response to children that reach for electric toys or giggle between handwashing and eating challa.

The challenge is to overcome not only an urge to use fear, but also our own lurking fears for our children. For example, while much of Shabbat observance involves abstaining from many of our typical weekday practices, we need to trust that our children will absorb this concept over time and that what is genuinely important to us will become important to them as well. Even though we can introduce the concepts of *muktze* and *melakha* at a young age and discuss them in our homes, I would suggest that we do not need to agonize or get involved when a three-year-old colors on Shabbat or turns on a musical toy. Unfortunately, though, fear, often subconscious, can lead us to unjustifiably rebuke or even punish a child in these circumstances, as we worry that this child does not, and therefore will not, care about Shabbat.

The concern is real, but this kind of reflexive response to it can be damaging in the long run. We can always teach our children more about the expectations of observance, but it is infinitely harder to undo negative feelings and associations. Rebuke and scolding may cause a child to quickly drop the crayon she was coloring with, but what feelings will be internalized at the same time? In her book *Off the Derech*, Faranak Margolese describes how being subjected to scare tactics as young children was often cited by Jews who abandoned Orthodoxy as one precipitating factor. To be sure, not every child who is yelled at for eating without a *berakha* will run away from Judaism, but the distaste can still leave its mark, and parents can benefit from being sensitive to the bigger picture.

## TRUSTING OUR VALUES

Moreover, fear is palpable and easily detected by even the youngest of children. If our youth sense fear, they might learn that even the adults in their lives don't authentically believe in the inherent attractiveness of the very tradition they are working to transmit. If, however, we trust the potency and vitality of our own values – that is, if we genuinely believe in the ancient power of Judaism itself – then we should trust that these values will penetrate over time. We will ultimately parent our children better, as we use situations as opportunities for education rather than for punishment. We need confidence that it is entirely possible to inculcate a strong belief system that is based on a perspective of trust.

**Shmuel: "Where Is Your *Kippa*?"**

*When we lived in the United States, our children attended an elementary school that attracted a wide spectrum of families. One Sunday, our son Shmuel, a first-grader at the time, asked for a playdate with his classmate Josh. When Josh arrived, we were a bit surprised to see that he was not wearing any head covering. While we were well aware that non-Orthodox families attended the yeshiva, we assumed that a child invited to a playdate at another family would keep to the same standards expected in school. My husband and I were curious to see how Shmuel, who noticed everything, would react.*

*At first, Shmuel did not seem to pay attention. Then, after Josh had already been in our home for a while, Shmuel suddenly looked up in the middle of a game and said, "Josh, where is your kippa?" Josh answered that in his family they do not wear kippot and tzitzit when they are at home. Shmuel contemplated that answer for a moment, then responded, "Oh, in my family we do wear kippot and tzitzit at home," and the two of them resumed playing.*

My husband and I were struck by this short exchange. We knew that in other circles, this conversation might constitute terrifying grounds for immediately pulling a child out of the school. We, though, were delighted and reassured to know that Shmuel was clearly confident and proud of his family's practices without being shaken by encountering something different. He did not respond with mocking or condescension. Learning that not everyone did as he did was cause for curiosity, but not arrogance or insecurity.

As Shmuel and our other children have grown, we have tried to stress our family's standards and beliefs from a place of pride and merit, rather than by disparaging alternative approaches. The goal is to develop their confidence in our/their approach without scaring them about the risks of other perspectives, on all sides. We hope that they will continue to feel good about themselves and their practices while still respecting and finding value in the diverse people around them, even if they completely disagree on many matters.

Trusting in our values is not limited only to external measures of religious standards and beliefs but can also include a range of other practices that are included in what it means to be a fully developed religious and dignified person. Values such as talking with respect, handling one's frustrations, and fulfilling one's responsibilities can also be reinforced with trust or through fear.

## A Personal Story: Disciplining Our Children

*As young parents, we believed that if a child of ours were not living up to our standards of behavior, then there must be an immediate consequence to make clear that we would not allow the infraction to go unnoticed. Looking back, I can see how many of the classic, underlying fears that prevent us from making good decisions were driving our parenting choices and reactions. Our self-perception was affected, as we were worried as to what it said about us as parents if our children did not always behave the way we expected. We were also aware that other people were looking both at us and at our children and thinking about and judging our parenting abilities. Finally, noticing and observing other families and their dynamics left us wondering if our struggles were normal and if we were the only ones with young children who were facing these challenges.*

As we gained more experience, consulted with parenting therapists, and developed more confidence in ourselves as parents, we began to understand that we could trust our instincts to choose to sometimes overlook a violation and not automatically respond to it. If parents trust that their children are well aware of their values, then they do not need to live in fear that every misdeed might mean that they have failed to educate their children properly. When we have faith in the power of our values and in the way we convey them to our children, we can better trust our intuitions about when to discipline and when to ignore, when to punish and when to let something go.

We do not need to act as policemen, holding our children accountable for every violation. We can feel confident that if we are positively educating toward our values, our children are internalizing them, even when they do not always appear to be. Sometimes we think a child is ignoring everything we tell him until we unexpectedly overhear him sharing with a friend a perspective of ours (that he had days earlier rolled his eyes at) or casually repeating a family value or rule to a younger sibling. These glimpses help build faith that our messages have penetrated.

## ENABLING INTERNALIZATION

Values are broader and deeper than specific concrete practices or consequences. The hope, therefore, is that children who are raised with firm, positive values will be able to access and apply these values in whatever situations they find themselves. As parents, we can feel less of a need to talk through every what-if scenario that can possibly arise. We can know that our children can be trusted to draw upon the values that are central to their upbringing and use them as a starting point, even when something unforeseen arises.

Our ultimate aspiration is that trusting our children will help them generate an internal yardstick that they will employ, even when on their own and when no punishment is at stake. Key to this is that children be taught that they can be trusted to know what is right and to make good decisions on their own. In this scenario, the perpetual motivating factor is belief in and allegiance to values that have been deeply inculcated. However, when fear is the motivator, and it either doesn't apply in a particular circumstance or can be overcome, adherence can hardly be expected.

Perhaps most importantly, trusting our children will empower them to trust their instincts even when others may question or doubt them. As parents, we want our children to be wary of people who do not inspire their trust and who they think can be hurtful or even dangerous. A child must be taught to pay attention to his or her inner radar and to those butterflies in the stomach, even when the person in question is someone highly respected. We want our children to take their own hesitations and concerns seriously and to be honest with themselves and with us about them. This ability is reinforced through the message that they can and should trust their judgments and assessments about the people and situations they encounter.

## TRUSTING THAT OUR CHILDREN LOVE US

A different kind of trust that parenting requires is the trust that our children will love us even if we need to discipline them. If parents are constantly in need of their children's affection and afraid that it could be damaged, weak parenting may ensue. By contrast, if parents maintain clear values and are consistent about educating toward them and gently enforcing their expression, children will hopefully develop respect for their parents for having principles. They may not enjoy following the rules in the moment, but if parents put faith in their own beliefs, then, with time and maturity, kids will hopefully come to trust those convictions as well.

## Chapter 18

# Mentoring and Educating with Trust

I frequently share with students the importance of education happening in an environment of trust rather than fear. Students, just as one's children, need to be given the tools to become life-long, independent learners, thinkers, and decision makers. Rather than training students to doubt their own intuitions and to turn elsewhere for guidance, teachers should empower them to exercise and respect their own ever-maturing judgments, at age appropriate levels. This section is directly relevant, therefore, not only to those who find themselves in a formal or informal mentoring position, but also to students themselves, as they stand to benefit from the ability to identify and seek out educators who strive to teach and guide from a place of trust.

## HEALTHY MENTORING

Students often seek out mentors when they are looking for advice and direction in making big decisions. A student can feel stuck in his or her own thinking and might come talk to a teacher with the goal of having someone older and wiser tell him or her what to do.

Personally, I am very reluctant to play this role when a student approaches me. I believe strongly that people can and should be trusted to know themselves best, as well as to intuit what is right for them (with the caveat that they are first willing to engage in honest reflection). I also believe that a person making a decision needs to be ready to fully own the consequences of that choice.

Therefore, the role of a mentor, as I understand it, is to help guide students in figuring out what they want. Critically, this process begins with careful listening on the part of the educator. *What is it that this student is trying to say? What are the motivating forces? Does fear seem to be a factor? Do the words being used and the sentiments being expressed make it clear what this person really wants? What appear to be the underlying issues and concerns? Is there a deeper question or struggle behind the dilemma that is being presented? Is there unhealthy or even pathological thinking that is guiding this decision-making process?*

Listening closely, reflecting back key statements, and asking relevant follow-up and clarifying questions can go a long way in encouraging a student to think carefully about what he or she is looking for. Sometimes, the listening and questioning shed light on aspects of an experience or thinking that the student himself is not fully aware of. Taking this reflective, listening approach can help a teacher verify that the student is thinking everything through, taking all factors into account, being honest about all parts of his or her processing, and is aware of the different consequences of a potential decision.

A teacher might also share his or her own general thoughts and perspectives about the issue at hand. After all that is done, however, the educator should step back and let the student reflect about what she thinks is best. When a student is encouraged to think something through on her own and to trust her own instincts, she will more likely make solid, considered, and educated decisions and will also feel more prepared to take responsibility for the effects they will have on her life.

Students don't always appreciate this approach in the moment. As they are struggling through tough life decisions or dealing with questions on their minds, they might pressure their mentors to tell them what to think. Sometimes they even want the decision made for them, if only to ease the burden of responsibility. Mentors should be exceedingly cautious about being put in this position and meeting this demand. While a mentor can and should be there to share thoughts and to raise ideas and even hesitations, in the long run, students will appreciate and benefit greatly from an education that empowers them to trust their own decision-making processes.

## FOSTERING INDEPENDENCE

This approach to decision making has implications not only for discrete, one-on-one episodes of counseling, but also for the overall culture of an educational institution. A healthy learning environment should respect the personal autonomy of its students and help them develop the skills, knowledge, and confidence necessary to be able to reach their own personal and halakhic decisions in the future. Of course, this includes teaching students to be genuinely self-aware and honest enough to sometimes arrive at the conclusion that they need to consult others who possess expertise.

As such, while I believe in the importance of fostering independence, I am certainly not advocating giving a false sense of confidence to students who aren't worthy of it. To the contrary, it is crucial that we teach boundaries and humility so that students are aware of their own limits and capabilities and can know how and when to use the resources available to them in their lives. What I am suggesting, however, is that the overall trajectory of education ought to aim for students' increasing independence and self-sufficiency rather than toward a tethered and uncertain existence. When students do turn to mentors, it should be out of an autonomous, confident choice to seek an outside opinion, rather than out of an acquired, reflexive anxiety about confronting life's challenges on one's own.

Caution, deliberateness, and prudence are fine to teach, but unease, confusion, and insecurity are not. In the short run, instilling these latter traits may encourage students to come running for their teachers' wisdom and approval at every turn, but in most cases the model is not sustainable. Students who grow increasingly dependent on the input of mentors are bound to be disappointed at some point when those mentors are unable to stay as invested and available as the students now need them to be. Not only will these students lack the skills to navigate life on their own, but they may also harbor resentment toward the mentors who nurtured their dependency but then moved on to the next crop of young minds.

Our students, even the most loyal, will not be with us forever, and helping them develop the ability to navigate life's difficult choices as responsible adults must be the ultimate goal of our efforts. At some point, we must give our students (just like our children) the tools with which to make the best decisions possible and then educate them to trust themselves to continue to learn and grow, even when they falter. To outsiders who measure the success of a teacher or institution based on rapid, external change, it might look like there is failure if a student doesn't always make the "expected" right decision. But those on the inside know how far someone has come, how much he or she has truly learned, what he or she has internalized, and what will last a lifetime.

## POSITIVITY IN THE GAP YEAR AND ALWAYS

More broadly, I would suggest that a spirit of optimism, encouragement, and patience should saturate the entirety of Torah education, never more so than in the post-high school phase. Instead of motivating growth through fear and guilt, strong religious education should lay out a positive vision of what one can aspire to – in Torah study, in *yirat Shamayim*, in *ahavat Hashem*, and in *shemirat hamitzvot*. Students should be taught that true and lasting growth is a slow and steady process and that it is not all or nothing. They should learn that small steps are meaningful and valued and that they ultimately lead us steadily and securely in the right direction. They should be shown that just because we have not yet reached the final destination doesn't mean that we should give up or be afraid, and they should be told that we can always keep growing and moving toward wherever we want to go.

Furthermore, an institution of learning that is founded upon trust and faith should be able to create an atmosphere in which students are comfortable being open and honest with their teachers about the struggles they experience. They should know and feel that they are viewed as individuals, each on his or her own path of continued personal and religious growth, moving along at his or her own unique pace.

When positive education is successful at fostering independence, there is ownership, there is buy-in, there is joy, and there is empowerment. There is also growth, maturity, and self-reflection. Additionally, when independence is valued, the connections that develop between students and teachers contain the potential to evolve into mutual adult relationships and are not frozen in time, stuck forever in the mentor-protégé dynamic.

This type of education requires respect, humility, responsibility, trust, patience, creativity, and hard work on the part of both the teacher and the student. It involves a shift from teaching for the next stage of life to teaching for a lifetime. The rewards, on all sides, are not as quickly and easily reaped, but they are ultimately much deeper and more satisfying than the easy payout of a quick turnaround.

## TEACHING HALAKHA WITH TRUST

The theme of trust has directly influenced my own teaching in other concrete ways. As a teacher of halakha, I try to demonstrate halakha's sophistication and sensitivity by exploring the primary halakhic texts with students and inviting them to understand the system from the inside. Halakha is rarely black-and-white, and, in teaching it, I do not think we should be afraid to show teenagers, or anyone else, the ambiguities and nuances of our tradition. Contrary to what one might expect, I have found that a trusting approach, when exercised cautiously, encourages students to appreciate the true nature of halakhot as well as their development. This appreciation then enables them to have greater respect for the system, for *poskim*, and for the different halakhic practices that they see around them.

Ultimately, my hope for students is that they grow into mature, sincere, and committed observers of halakha who are not suspicious of people who do things differently than they do. I pray that they, along with my own children, develop a deep understanding of and confidence in the ways they practice their religion without needing to be fearful of others. I think that when halakha, as well as Judaism in general, is presented from this perspective, it becomes even more attractive and worthy of pride.

## TRANSPARENCY

Sometimes, I find that this approach is initially confusing for students. When teaching halakha, I have had students express surprise that I don't close each topic with a bottom line of exactly what to do. Instead, I teach the halakhic sources and lay out the spectrum of interpretations that produce a range of possible conclusions. Especially when I teach a sensitive topic such as modesty in dress, there are always students who are expecting and waiting for me to disclose my own personal standards to the class. When I do not and instead leave the conclusions more open, they approach me, frustrated that I did not tell everyone what I personally believe is "the right way to dress." They are worried that their peers will end up doing less than they could have, had I laid out a more stringent, hard-line approach.

For this reason, I take time to explain to the class my educational philosophy of teaching from trust. First, I tell students that it would not be intellectually honest to teach that there is only one halakhic approach to a sensitive topic if that is not truly the case. Not only is it not honest, but it is also potentially dangerous. If a student later comes across sources that I chose not to mention in class, she can begin to doubt, rightfully, whether she can trust anything that I taught her. Was my goal to teach a topic or to encourage one specific, narrow outcome?

Additionally, the goal of education should not be to produce clones of the teacher. A teacher must operate with an awareness that every student sitting in a classroom comes from a different background, where various halakhic approaches may have been relied upon or where halakhic standards may not have been a priority at all. As a result, not all students may be struggling with or capable of attaining the same level of observance, and one standard might not be right for everyone. Presenting the diversity of opinions allows each student to understand that the halakha is not monolithic. At the very least, one can then begin to consider following a standard that he or she may not have been willing to entertain before.

Teaching in this style also gives students the ability to look around and respect a variety of practices. Even if a student follows one approach, she will now know what lies within the range of mainstream opinions and therefore will be able to acknowledge the validity of practices which differ from her own.

Moreover, this student will also understand the possibility of adapting or adjusting one's practice in the future. Life is long, and people find themselves in diverse circumstances as life progresses. What seemed impossible for someone at one point in time might appear doable only a few years down the line. On the other hand, what seemed easy and obvious in the past may now be more difficult. If the full halakhic spectrum is presented, a student will hopefully be able to continue to explore various halakhic options even as life evolves. This approach toward halakhic education aims to inspire and empower students to grow and strive for high standards while also trusting them to handle the complexities of life.

### FEAR AS A DETRIMENTAL MOTIVATOR

Unfortunately, sometimes well-meaning educators use fear as a motivator. In the moment, fear is quite powerful, and the short-term results can be impressive. If the outcome is positive, we might think that perhaps it is OK and even beneficial to draw on fear tactics. The question, however, is what happens down the road as a result of this technique. One particular story comes to mind:

### Rachel: On Fire...for a Day

*Rachel, a second-year student studying in Israel, approached me in tears, asking if we could talk. After a few attempts, she finally succeeded in telling me that even though all the first-year students looked up to her and thought of her as religiously committed, she had not davened in months and was not motivated to try. Indeed, this revelation was surprising, given the image that Rachel presented. We began to talk, and I asked Rachel what she thought had led her to stop davening, especially since daily tefilla had not been a struggle for her in the past.*

*As she started to think and reflect on the past few months, she began to describe a shiur she had heard toward the beginning of the year. She paused midsentence and admitted that before this conversation, she had not given much thought to this shiur or even consciously remembered it.*

*The shiur she suddenly flashed back to had been about tefilla and had inspired and moved her at the time in a way that had felt life-changing. The speaker spoke about how important it is to realize that when you are davening, you are really speaking to Hashem, and to do your best to concentrate intently on each word. He then concluded, "And if someone can't muster up the ability to know that she is talking to the Master of the World, if someone can say words and not even think about the fact that she is standing before the Creator as she says them, then there is no point in that conversation at all! Why bother to speak when you don't even know with whom you are speaking?"*

*Indeed, this was an enormously powerful and inspiring message – at least in the moment. Rachel described how her tefilla the next day was on a higher level than anything she had ever experienced before. But in the months that followed, as she could not maintain that concentration, she was left fearing that her davening meant nothing. This subconscious fear that had been planted within her slowly did its damage, until she stopped davening altogether.*

What is remarkable is the way that fear can suddenly confuse us about the things that we intuitively know well. Until that point, Rachel, along with lots of other observant Jews, davened daily, sometimes with more intent and sometimes with less. Though she might not have been able to articulate it, her practice stemmed from both an acknowledgment that the intensity of religious experience will naturally vary and an assumption that God is somehow accepting, or at least forgiving, of that reality. That is the Judaism that she had imbibed in her home and community. Yet, being afraid about the possibility of disingenuousness, Rachel forgot all that – at least until she received reassurance that she is normal and can trust the authenticity of her religious efforts.

Similarly, sometimes gap-year programs in Israel end with talks in which students are told that they must commit to learning a certain amount of Torah each day or to never missing a *minyan.* If they do not maintain these practices, they are warned, their spiritual worlds and their connection to Judaism will dry up.

It is indeed important to strive to make time each day to learn Torah. This message, though, can and should be given over as a value that we believe in and want to encourage. When it is connected to fear (however legitimately afraid the educator may be), a big risk is now introduced. There is potential for the message to backfire, as the fear becomes self-fulfilling:

- *A busy college student in the middle of finals finds that she went two days without learning anything. She is now convinced that she is in a downward spiral that she cannot control.*
- *Another student sleeps late and misses minyan one morning. Instead of getting up the next day and going as usual, he now sees himself as having fallen off the cliff he was warned about.*

We can certainly educate toward learning and davening and other practices and tell our students how crucial they are to our daily lives. But we must believe, and convince our students, that neither they nor these values will be instantly lost if they lag behind here and there. We must empower our students to trust that even if they sometimes fall short, they can pick up and keep going – because there is no other option.

## INCULCATING TRUST REQUIRES HUMILITY AND RESPECT

Finally, actively inculcating trust requires deep humility on the part of the teacher, as well as the resultant ability to genuinely respect one's students.

Humility allows us to understand and accept that each person is an individual, that it is important for students to cultivate that individuality and not suppress it, and that the goal is not to create miniature versions of ourselves. Teachers should give students the emotional and intellectual room to develop themselves and not overcrowd young minds with their own charisma. Furthermore, when mentors are ready and willing to share their own doubts, failings, and limitations, students learn that their role models, too, are human but nevertheless navigate life's challenges, and therefore so can they.

Humility on the part of teachers and acceptance of students' individuality enable teachers to better respect each of their students, and the students to better respect and trust themselves. Respecting students includes wanting to understand and appreciate where they come from and who they are. Students need to feel that their teachers value them, view them as trustworthy human beings, and don't trivialize their upbringings, interests, or relationships. Students should be spoken to with respect and not be patronized or belittled. If we are blessed with success in our effort to instill this self-trust in our students, they will hopefully develop into adults who not only are confident, independent, and self-respecting, but who can in turn encourage and nurture others to trust themselves as well.

*Chapter 19*

# Sharing Trust in Friendships and Relationships

$B$eing attuned to the concepts of trust and fear and how they impact our decision making and day-to-day lives can be useful in the context of friendships and relationships as well. Many times, a friend or spouse may turn to us for guidance or help in making a difficult decision. Of course, we should never be looking to mentor our peers in the same overt way we would a child or a student. But how, then, can we sensitively and effectively give advice or encouragement to those who are closest to us without it being inappropriate or condescending?

Many of the same general principles that we discussed regarding mentoring are significant here as well, but they require a different tone when it comes to peers. The wisest option, I think, when a friend confides in us and seeks advice is to first listen closely with deep humility and respect. Humility allows us to remain open to hearing someone else's perspective and approach without automatically and immediately thinking that we know better how to handle a given situation. Respecting the person before us is essential in order to put ourselves in his or her shoes and to appreciate his or her specific dilemma and thought process.

Close and active listening enables us to hear the issues and concerns that are being raised and discussed. Often, what someone really wants to do can become apparent quite quickly just by hearing and noticing which wants are being motivated by fear and which are not. Being sensitive to these factors and drawing someone's attention to them can be beneficial in giving the support and validation that is sought. Sometimes just listening, being sincerely caring and attentive, and reflecting back what we are hearing can be enough to give a peer the space and encouragement necessary to come to his or her own conclusions.

To be sure, each relationship has its own dynamic. For example, spouses, unlike friends, share a life, and therefore they need to work even harder to listen openly without imposing their own feelings on one another. Still, the basic principles of active, empathic listening are always relevant.

### Ayelet and Jason: Unexpected Changes at Work

*Ayelet walked out of a difficult meeting with her boss and called her husband Jason in tears. Jason was in the middle of his workday, but from the minute he picked up the phone, he could hear the distress in Ayelet's voice. He left his desk and walked outside so that he could give her his full attention. "I can't believe what she is asking from me," Ayelet sobbed into the phone. "She said that if I want to remain full time at this office, I need to increase my workweek by at least six hours." Ayelet was livid. She began listing to Jason all the reasons why she should quit.*

*Jason listened carefully and patiently. He knew that Ayelet was upset and had been caught off guard, but he also knew how much she loved her job, her colleagues, and her work environment. Jason validated her frustration and anger and told her that he would support whatever decision she made. But before they hung up, he added,*

*"I know this is a really tough and unexpected situation, but it is also important to make sure you think carefully about whether you really want to actually leave. Do you want to go out and find new work, given this upsetting change? Or, despite the frustrations, do you still want to be there?"*

The role of a friend or spouse, similar to that of a mentor, is never to tell someone what to do, but instead to help the person figure out what it is she wants for herself. In this case, Ayelet was not really interested in leaving her workplace and looking for a new job, and Jason knew that. She was thrown by the conversation with her boss and disappointed by the change in conditions, yet she knew deep inside that she was happy at work and wanted to stay nonetheless. After Jason listened, respected her feelings, gave her the space to vent, and validated her, he was able to empower her to make a good decision by simply reminding her to think about what she really wanted.

This wasn't easy, as Jason knew that her decision, either way, would have repercussions for him and for their family. But he took a deep breath and tried to remember that this is what Ayelet needed from him in the moment, and that is what he would want from her as well.

In short, we empower our peers and spouses by gently reminding them that they can trust themselves and their assessment of a situation. At the same time, friends might turn to us because they trust that we will let them know if they are overreacting, if something doesn't sound right or if we are hearing fear in their analyses. They hope they can rely on a good and close friend to look out for their interests, even as he or she will give them space to think through the situation for themselves.

### Nava: Dealing with a Difficult Parent
*Nava was in her late forties and the mother of five grown children, but that didn't mean she was beyond dealing with a difficult relationship with her own mother. Nava's mother was not an easy woman. She*

could grow irritated without warning and was quick to lose patience and take out her frustration on those around her. From the time Nava was little, she had borne the brunt of her mother's bad moods and had often been blamed for things that were not her fault. As Nava matured, she realized what a negative impact this had on her psyche and had sought out professional help in navigating the complex emotions that swirled within her. After much hard work, she had managed to get to a healthier place where she was able to draw necessary and appropriate boundaries in their relationship.

Throughout her life, Nava had turned to her best friend Risa to discuss her challenging situation. She knew that Risa really understood all the dynamics and was able to help her process the wide and complex range of feelings that would arise. Now, Nava picked up the phone to call Risa and share her mother's request to come stay with her for two months. Usually, when her mother came to visit, she rented a nearby apartment. Minutes ago, however, she had announced to Nava her desire to stay in Nava's house so that she could "have maximum time with the grandchildren." Nava told Risa that she was scared to say no because she knew that her mother would not be happy and would likely subject Nava to another rant about what a horrible and uncaring daughter she was.

Risa listened to everything Nava shared and let her discuss whatever was on her mind. After hearing it all and validating all of her frustrations, Risa suggested that Nava consider what she really wanted and what she thought would be the best decision under the circumstances.

Risa knew how challenging it would be for Nava to have her mother in her home, but she also knew that she could not and did not want to make the final decision for her. She could, though, reflect back to Nava the fear she heard in her voice and encourage her to stay focused on what she ultimately wanted and knew would be best.

For her part, Nava appreciated Risa's empathy and the fact that she never told Nava what to do. Risa's approach gave Nava the strength to confront her mother and protect her own needs, even knowing full well what she would have to endure in the process. Nava was so grateful to have a friend like Risa in her life. She also knew to be careful not to overburden Risa, become too dependent on her, or take for granted the time or support Risa gave her.

Sometimes the most meaningful thing we can do for a friend who is in the process of making a difficult decision is to just let the person know that we are confident he or she will find a way forward and make good choices. Hearing this and being reminded of its truth can be incredibly empowering and uplifting on its own.

*Chapter 20*

# Trust in Ourselves

$O$f course, the most crucial kind of trust (and a corollary to trust in God) is trust in oneself, which is the key to being able to make any good decision. Faith in God and the free will which He grants us includes the faith that we are empowered to make good decisions. When we trust ourselves, we can breathe easier, because we know that at any given moment in time, we are capable of making the best next move to get us toward the next place we want to go.

Over time, this trust can grow, as we look back on our track record of decisions and can better assess what went well and what did not. This reflection informs our future decisions and bolsters the confidence we need to trust in God's assurance that we will be prepared to handle any situation that comes our way.

Here are some key components that can enable us to trust ourselves more.

## TRUST IN OUR ABILITY TO COPE

### A Personal Story: Dealing with Terror

*It was the winter of 2016, and Israel was in the midst of a spate of awful, lone-wolf terror attacks. Barely a day went by without news of another horrific stabbing or car ramming. Among the victims were people we or our friends knew. It was hard to function without worrying about who would be next. When I said goodbye to my children and husband in the morning, I could not stop the thought of "Will we all return home at the end of this day?" from entering my mind.*

*One evening, I shared my ruminations with a psychologist friend. "What's your biggest fear?" she asked me.*

*"That something will happen to Judah, and I'll be left on my own," I answered.*

*"And then what would happen?" she continued.*

*"I would be devastated. I wouldn't be able to manage. I would miss him terribly. I'd be a single parent."*

*"And then what would happen?" she pushed further.*

*"I guess I would figure out how to move forward because I would have to. I would have no other choice."*

The minute I heard those words come out of my mouth, I began to feel a little better. I had confronted my worst fear and realized that somehow, as awful as it would be, life would continue. Just as I have managed so many situations in the past – admittedly with difficulties and missteps along the way – I suddenly felt able to trust that I would somehow figure out how to navigate that unimaginable possibility as well.

While our fears can be terrifying, realizing that we can trust ourselves to respond is empowering and liberating. We do not have to live in fear. Although life may throw us curveballs and we may encounter incredibly challenging situations that we did not anticipate, we can trust that we will have the necessary tools to handle them in the best way possible. We have resilience, and we have the ability to make the best next decision at each step along the way.

**CORE VALUES**

Another part of developing trust in oneself is formulating and cementing our core values. These are the values that we identify as so important to us in life that we want to carry them forward with us always, no matter where we find ourselves and no matter what life brings our way. Examples of core values can include relationships with family or friends, connection to *tefilla* or to Torah, living a healthy lifestyle, or the place of *ḥesed* or the Land of Israel in our lives.

On the one hand, for each of our core values, there should be concrete manifestations which are non-negotiable, so basic to us that they will always be incorporated into our lives, no matter what. At the same time, if we know what our core values are, we can trust that as we navigate life we will figure out how to bring these values to expression in every situation.

### Nechama: Too Far Gone?

*Nechama had returned from her seminary year in Israel passionate about and committed to tefilla. Not only had she decided that she would daven three times a day, but she also put a lot of time and effort into each Amida prayer. Now, at the age of twenty-seven and with three children and a full-time job, Nechama found that she was often rushing through davening and that on some days she would forget to daven Minḥa or Maariv. A couple of times, an entire day had even gone by without her davening at all. Nechama could not believe what had happened to her. How could it be that she had fallen so far from where she had been? The only way that she could make sense of it was to admit to herself that she clearly no longer valued tefilla the way she once did.*

When Nechama left seminary, she thought of *tefilla* as a specific commitment to davening three times a day and always with a tremendous amount of concentration. Instead of thinking of *tefilla* as a core value in her life, Nechama equated it with a particular practice. But when this became increasingly difficult to sustain, Nechama fearfully concluded that she must no longer care about the value itself.

In reality, the circumstances of Nechama's life had evolved quickly and dramatically within a short period of time. It is likely that she still identifies with and cares about the purpose and role of *tefilla* in her life, but she does not have the same time and headspace to daven the way that she used to. Instead of rechanneling her connection to *tefilla* into a modification of her previous practice, she assumes that *tefilla* is no longer relevant to her in any way.

Alternatively, a woman who has identified a core value of *tefilla* may say, "No matter what, I always want *tefilla* to be a part of my life." This may mean different things for different people at different points. While someone may see davening three times a day as basic to her life and utterly non-negotiable, another woman may see davening once a day as her red line, while a third woman may decide that "a conversation with God," even if it is not formal *tefilla*, is something she will not compromise on.

Basic, non-negotiable commitments within a core value should always be present. But at the same time, we can accept that other details may vary based on time, place, and situation. How long are my *tefillot*? How much *kavana* do I have? Will I daven with a *minyan*? How many times a day will I daven? Over time, the answers to these questions may change, and there might be varying expressions of values. The hope, though, is that the core values themselves will remain constant. Furthermore, our range of core values might expand over time.

When we stay deeply aware of our values, we can feel good that there is consistency in who we are, what is important to us, and what we prioritize. At the same time, we can be confident that there is constant growth and thought about how to apply those values to our ever-changing situations.

Nechama is scared. She knows that she should probably reformulate her practical commitment to *tefilla*, but she is terrified that this amounts to admitting defeat. For now, her fear is keeping her tenuously tied to her old ways, but she feels duplicitous and empty and doubts that this will last. But there is another way out. If she can learn to trust, return to, and invest in her core value of *tefilla*, she is likely to come out davening more, not less.

## FAMILY AND FRIENDS

Trusting ourselves is crucial, but we don't always have to shoulder that burden alone. Family and friends can be our greatest anchors in life, especially when we are able to depend on them to honestly reflect with us about where we are and how we are doing. It can be helpful at any station in life to have people to turn to whom we really trust, respect, and admire. They should be people who share or appreciate our core values, know what we want in life, and are willing to help us hold ourselves to those standards. Ironically, part of trusting ourselves is knowing that we have surrounded ourselves with figures to whom we can turn for a different perspective, who can help us process what it is we are looking for, and who can ensure that we stay on track to achieve the goals that we have set out to accomplish.

As we discussed in chapter 19, friends who know how to listen carefully with great humility and respect can be tremendous resources as we navigate life and seek out perspective and guidance. They know us well, have our best interests in mind, and can be insightful in helping us figure out what it is we want and how to achieve it.

Sometimes, we might have an intuitive sense of when we need to turn to someone for guidance or reassurance. At the same time, we worry that if we are truly independent and successful, then we should be able to move forward without having to lean on others. Asking for help may feel weak or reflect anxiety.

Paradoxically, however, sometimes it is our fears which push us to "be brave." We try to use self-sufficiency to overcome insecurity.

Ultimately, though, we face the same question: What do we really want? What do we genuinely believe will serve us best and help us succeed? Rather than doubt or repress our instinct to reach out to someone, we should trust that we know when it is useful to look beyond ourselves to the people in our lives who provide us with insight and strength.

PART IV

# After the Decision...
# Now What?

## Chapter 21

# Developing Confidence in Our Decisions

Learning to make decisions from a place of trust can take time and hard work, but when this skill is developed and employed, the resulting empowerment is well worth the effort. If we carefully examine all sides of an issue and work through the various elements discussed and demonstrated throughout this book, hopefully our gut instincts about what we want and our abilities to be attuned to them will become stronger and more straightforward. We will more clearly identify underlying motivators and more easily arrive at good decisions. That doesn't mean, however, that we will never doubt ourselves. Often, even after we know that we have made a good decision from a place of trust and not from fear, we may still wonder if our intuitions and decisions are trustworthy. Here are several reasons why we should feel good about trusting our gut instincts:

## WE ARE THE BEST ONES TO HAVE
## MADE THIS DECISION

No one is better positioned to have made a good decision for ourselves than we are. We are the ones who know ourselves best. We have intimate knowledge of our strengths and weaknesses, our likes and dislikes, and our past successes and failures. Therefore, we are uniquely suited to weigh all of the different aspects of a decision and to think about them from our specific perspective. We have the most experience with what works and what doesn't work for us. We have learned and gained insight from our past decisions about what it is that we want. We can trust our instincts that we are doing what makes sense for us and that we have come to conclusions that will continue to make us feel good.

## WE DID EXTENSIVE RESEARCH AND
## STILL CHOSE THIS OPTION

Before coming to our decision, we took all the issues into account. We gathered information and spoke to different people who understand the situation from the inside. Perhaps we even made a pros-and-cons list. We thought and rethought and came to the point where there is no factor of this decision that we did not thoroughly consider. Trust means knowing that if we feel we want to proceed in a particular direction, even after we have listed all of our concerns and have honestly admitted everything that frightens us about them, then we must really want this. It explains why we made this decision, and it means a lot, because we are the ones who will have to live with the consequences of the decisions we make.

## GOD BELIEVES IN US

God created each of us with the ability to make our own choices (*behira hofshit*). As such, He necessarily believes deeply in our capability to do so. He wants us to make good decisions, and He must trust that we can. If He created us as independent, autonomous beings, He must have given us the tools that we need to think about what makes the most sense for us.

Sometimes, as in my conversation with a friend about traveling to America for a *simḥa* (chapter 2), I will hear the comment that the best way to make a decision is to think about what God would want us to do (*ratzon Hashem*). While I agree completely with the importance of considering what God's will is, this line of reasoning, as we mentioned earlier, will not always get us so far.

When faced with a moral choice between apparently good and bad, reflecting upon God's will can help propel us in the right direction. However, many of the most difficult decisions that we confront are between two good, complex options that are starkly different from one another and that offer different benefits for us. Since, in these cases, we have no absolute way of knowing what God would want of us, we have no choice but to use the abilities, insight, and self-awareness that He gave us to make the best decisions that we can.

Even if some individuals naturally turn to Torah sages for insight into *ratzon Hashem*, that, too, is a decision, as is how, when, whom to consult, and in what circumstances. Ultimately, there is no escaping responsibility for our choices, and thus the need for faith in a God-given ability to make good decisions.

As I see it, this faith is an outgrowth of genuine faith in Hashem's guarantee of *beḥira ḥofshit*. He assures us that we will always have the ability to choose well; we will never be denied the insight that we need. If Hashem empowers us and puts His faith in us, then I believe we ought to feel comfortable and confident trusting in ourselves and our decisions as well.

## WE HAVE LEARNED FROM OUR PAST DECISIONS

When looking back at various crossroads in our lives, if we find that for the most part we are happy with the decisions we have made and with where they have led us, that helps us build trust in ourselves and in our decision-making abilities. If we are living with gnawing doubts after a challenging, gut-wrenching decision, we can recall that the decisions we have made in the past have brought us to this point in life, and we can trust that, once again, we have chosen wisely.

Even if we regret a decision we have made, the fact that we are able to recognize that and can change course accordingly is highly significant. In Tractate Berakhot (34b) we are told that "the place which the penitent occupy, the perfectly righteous are unable to occupy." Why is this so? Perhaps because those who have repented and changed their ways have learned much from those experiences. They have an ability to move forward and grow from their new understandings in a different and more powerful way than someone who has never had to remake herself and start anew. Similarly, even a "bad" decision, when reexamined from the right perspective, can ultimately result in our being able to trust ourselves more. The experience of earnestly regretting a decision can actually help us better understand what our current needs are and how we want to proceed from here.

## WE WILL ENSURE OUR OWN SUCCESS

If we decide to do something because we want to, we will do everything in our power to ensure that we succeed. Even when things get tough, we will not be afraid, because we knew all along what the drawbacks of this decision were, yet, despite them, we decided that we wanted to move ahead with this choice anyway. This recognition and understanding leave us better prepared to navigate any challenge that will come our way.

By contrast, if a decision is made from a place of fear and we decide to do something that we don't really want to do, the result can be resentment, frustration, and even anger when we find ourselves in a situation that we didn't proactively choose. Instead of feeling ready to make the most of where we are, the lingering emotion may be, "Why am I dealing with this? I am only here because I was afraid to do what I really wanted," and then we may feel stuck. While fears and an honest confrontation with reality naturally play a big part in every decision, they should not be the determining factor behind a decision when we find ourselves drawn to an alternative. We can trust that if the fear is significant enough, it will naturally change what it is that we want.

## WE WILL TAKE RESPONSIBILITY MOVING FORWARD

When we take responsibility for our decisions and realize that we made the choices that brought us to where we are today, we better understand that if we are not happy with where we find ourselves, it is within our power to make a change.

Rabbi Jonathan Sacks *zt"l* often shared the story of an exchange that he had in his formative years with the Lubavitcher Rebbe. When Rabbi Sacks opened with the words, "In the situation in which I find myself," the Rebbe interrupted him and said, "You do not *find* yourself in a situation. You *place* yourself in a situation; and if you placed yourself in one, you can place yourself in another" (Jonathan Sacks, *The Great Partnership: God, Science and the Search for Meaning*, 91).

Similarly, we sometimes tell ourselves that we *had* to do something. But most often, we *chose* to do something because of myriad factors. When we use the language of "had," it can be a sign that we are afraid of taking responsibility for a bad decision. But that relinquishing of responsibility makes it harder to admit our mistakes and consider changing direction.

If, however, we are ready to take responsibility for and own our decisions, then we can always ask ourselves if we chose from trust or fear, if we are happy with the results, and if we want to shift course. If we feel we made a decision from fear and we are upset about that, we can admit our mistake and reexamine the decision anew. If we feel regret over a decision that we made because we have new information, feelings, or perspective on the situation, then we can acknowledge that circumstances have changed and make the **best next decision** moving forward.

## WE CAN TRUST OUR INSTINCTS

Our inner voice is extraordinarily strong. If we give ourselves the right input and the room to hear it, that inner voice often rises up and lets us know what we want to do at the right time. Asking ourselves, "But what do you *want* to do?" as opposed to wondering what others want for us or what we think we should want for ourselves is a powerful way of making and feeling good about our decisions.

Feeling trust in ourselves and taking responsibility for our own decisions is an empowering and liberating experience. Rather than try to describe it in my own words, let me quote from an email I once received from a former student after a conversation we had about a significant decision:

*After I got off the phone with you yesterday (it's a bit embarrassing, but I'll tell you), I played music on my computer and just danced. Literally, by myself in a college dorm room, just dancing. I felt this sense of empowerment that I can trust myself! It just changed the way I see things, made me realize A LOT about myself and the reason why I often do certain things (like ask every person I know what they think before I make the decision because if there is a RIGHT answer, then they can help me get to that RIGHT answer and help me see things that I don't see instead of just looking inward and thinking about what I want). I still don't know what I want but I'm hoping I'll realize soon. This approach was refreshing to hear and really made me think.*

*Chapter 22*

# Living with Tension

$F$inally, trusting ourselves to make good decisions also means trusting that we are strong enough to live with tension. Even after we make the best decision we can, it is possible to still feel tension concerning it. It is not easy to live with tension, but sometimes it is necessary, and I believe it is often crucial. When we recognize that our decisions are often between two wonderful but different options, we can appreciate the normal tension that arises in needing to let go of one appealing possibility as we move forward with another. To deny the tension we experience as a result is to simplify things, to erase the complexity of human experience, and to wish away the conflicting values that pull at us in opposite directions.

It is possible to find incredible meaning and happiness through living with tension despite the inherent difficulty involved. Living with tension means that we are always evaluating and balancing different values that we believe in deeply and are not willing to sacrifice. That in and of itself is something to take tremendous pride in and contributes much meaning to our lives.

There are all kinds of tensions that we may deal with, such as: conflicting feelings about our careers or where to settle down, tensions around ideological and religious issues, ruminations about different elements of a relationship, and conflicting interests about our life pursuits. If we are able to make good decisions from a place of trust while still acknowledging the tensions that we feel, then we can continue to hold onto the various underlying values that are important to us. This means moving forward with the option we most want while being honest at the same time about what we are giving up, acknowledging both the price we are paying and the sadness that may come along with it.

If we can muster this emotional strength, then we are more likely to maintain the multiple values in our lives and to find other ways to express those that appear to have been momentarily suspended with any particular decision. If, on the other hand, we are not honest about or can't handle the tension and try to suppress or deny one side of our feelings, we may end up irrecoverably sacrificing something that was valuable and meaningful to us.

At the root of the tension that is sometimes felt in the wake of a concrete decision is "cognitive dissonance," a concept I first learned about in my psychology classes in college. Cognitive dissonance is the psychological stress experienced when one tries to maintain multiple conflicting ideas or values that are not easily resolvable, or when one acts in a way that seems to run counter to a deeply held belief. The stress that results from feeling pulled in different directions is deeply uncomfortable and drives us to seek to reconcile the conflicting feelings we are experiencing.

Here, though, lies yet another choice. If we respond by instinctively letting go of one of our values or changing our beliefs so that they wholly line up with and justify our actions, the tension will disappear, but so might a significant piece of us along with it. This is a reaction from fear – fear of psychological discomfort – and in the long run it might not reflect what we really want.

But there is an alternative. We can embrace tension, and even a dose of discomfort, without fear. We can accept that life is complicated, even confusing, and that there are competing values that clash with each other and can't always be mutually satisfied. We can trust ourselves to be capable of owning the decisions that we make and of explaining them to ourselves, rather than fear confronting what they might reveal about who we really are.

Trusting ourselves and our ability to make good decisions means accepting the complexities of life and even of our own character. It means building and maintaining positive narratives about ourselves and believing in our own genuineness and capacity for honesty with ourselves. It means staring down fears of duplicity and hypocrisy and overcoming them. Ultimately, with trust, we can confront the inherent stress of cognitive dissonance and resolve it in ways that are not so harsh or exacting.

Remember Nechama and her *tefilla* crisis in chapter 20? How she thought she must no longer care about davening because she struggled as a young mother to maintain her commitment to three intense *tefillot* each day? Perhaps she can be encouraged to reframe her evolution over time. Perhaps she hasn't lost her passion and idealism or settled for a mediocre religious life; rather, she is juggling the competing values of acting with selflessness for her young family with her own need for personal growth and religious fulfillment. Even if she is not davening as she was in seminary, she doesn't have to renounce her commitment to *tefilla* in order to make sense of herself. She can affirm the value of *tefilla* in her life but accept that other responsibilities take priority right now. Her children will not be little forever, though, and if she holds on to her value of *tefilla*, it may yet blossom again. If, however, she finds the tension too uncomfortable and jumps to redefine herself and her relationship with God, something precious may be tragically lost forever.

*Conclusion*

# Get Out There and Live!

I̤t is wonderful to be able to live and operate from a place of trust. We can believe in ourselves and in our ability to make good choices and to know what we want, even when the situation and the resulting consequences carry much weight. This attitude can be life changing on many different levels.

When it comes to overwhelming and consequential decisions that we face, trust gives us the necessary confidence to go with what we intuitively feel is right. Trust allows us to focus on making only the best next decision, because we can rely on ourselves to continually do exactly that at every stage. Trust also enables us to own our decisions and take responsibility for them, knowing that we actively chose our path after deliberate consideration of all the possible outcomes.

Trust, though, can also affect our day-to-day, smaller choices. Developing trust can revolutionize the way that we think about and approach even the trivial decisions that we constantly encounter in our lives.

### Ilana: Coffee or Latte?

*Ilana was a loyal customer of Starbucks. Every day on her way to work she stopped there for her order of regular coffee. She savored every drop of it and looked forward to starting each workday with her cup in hand.*

*On her birthday, however, Ilana found herself suddenly stressed about which coffee to buy. On the one hand, Ilana really looked forward to and thoroughly enjoyed her regular order. On the other hand, Starbucks had a birthday special that allowed a customer to order any drink for free.*

*"Should I go for the six dollar special latte that I would otherwise never allow myself to splurge on? What if I am just in the mood for my usual boring (and much cheaper) coffee? But how can I pass up the opportunity to get something different and more expensive?" she thought to herself.*

*Ilana could not believe the amount of time she spent thinking about what to do. "Why am I letting this decision weigh on me so heavily?" she wondered. "It's just coffee!"*

What Ilana decides to do in the end does not matter as much as why she decides. If she decides to get her regular coffee, despite the unique opportunity of the birthday special, it should be because her regular coffee is ultimately what she wants to savor that morning. Conversely, if she orders the special latte, hopefully it is because that is what she is in the mood for and she is excited at the prospect of trying something new and different. If she gets the latte only because she fears missing out on the opportunity for a special drink, she will likely regret it later when she craves her familiar, boring coffee.

Situations and decisions like this abound in life:

- *Should my husband and I walk out of a movie we are not enjoying, even though we don't want to feel that we wasted money on the tickets?*
- *Should I wear the dress that I feel good in when I go to interview,*

even though I am worried that it might not be sophisticated enough?

- Should I have the shawarma that I want for lunch, even though I am nervous about dairy then being off-limits for the next six hours?
- Should I shop at the convenient local grocery store and save myself valuable time, even though I know that the items are sometimes overpriced, and I don't want to feel taken advantage of?
- Should I go to sleep at a reasonable hour, even when I worry that I have not had a productive enough day?

Once we are sensitive to the "fear versus trust" dichotomy, we will find it popping up in many different areas of life. We can be more aware regarding what drives our behavior and our decisions. We can check to see if we are being motivated by fear or by trust, even when it comes to little choices. We can think proactively about consequences, benefits, and costs. And we can learn to listen to our inner voice more clearly.

Trusting ourselves means knowing that whatever stands before us, we are up for the task. We can do the research when necessary, collect the information we need, and weigh the pros and cons of each side. We can be honest about the impending consequences and take responsibility for the choices we make. Most importantly, each of us can look in the mirror and ask ourselves, directly and without fear: **What do you really want?** ... and trust that we will eventually know the answer.

*Maggid Books*
*The best of contemporary Jewish thought from*
*Koren Publishers Jerusalem Ltd.*